Tales From
Porcupine Junction
(A Moose Pasture Paradise)

The motto of Porcupine Junction:

*"If you think you're too small
to make a difference,
you haven't been in bed with a mosquito."*

Clare McCarthy

Published by
Mac Press,
30 Elm Ave., Orangeville,
ON Canada L9W 3G4

All illustrations by Clare McCarthy
Photos of Clare by Gus Dickson
Cover Design and Photographs by Gus Dickson

ISBN 978-0-9877826-2-5

10 9 8 7 6 5 4 3 2 1

Tales From Porcupine Junction (A Moose Pasture Paradise)

Clare McCarthy

All aspects of the community of Porcupine Junction are fictitious, but like a swarm of northern mosquitoes, elements of the truth at times settle in, during the telling of this tale.

This story is timeless, but is probably inspired by events which took place, more-or-less, during the middle of the 20th Century.

Dedicated to the Northern Ontario hamlet of Gold Centre, my birthplace, and inspiration for this novel.

Clare McCarthy

Table of Contents

1. Porcupine Junction 1

2. Bert's Fix-It Shop 9

3. The Moose Hunters 23

4. A Village Comes To Life 35

5. Awaiting The Results 61

6. Breaking News 83

7. Not Your Average Farmer 91

8. Martin Eagle Claw 119

9. The Fall Harvest Time 135

10. Blow, Blow, Thou Winter
     Winds 155

11. A Season Of Challenges 163

12. Gettin' The Year Off To A
     Good Start 173

13. It's Going To Be A Scorcher ... 179

14. Whistling In The Wilderness ... 193

15. On A Wing And A Prayer 197

More Table of Content

16. The Four Horsemen of the
        Apocalypse 219
17. It Ain't Over 'Til It's Over ... 225
18. Who Would'a Thunk it? 231
19. In The Wake of Change 235
20. The Final Word 243
Mac, A Mini-Biography 247
Acknowledgments 251

1

Porcupine Junction

Where Life is not a spectator sport

The Northern Ontario Hamlet of Porcupine Junction sat like a contented bullfrog on the shore of Moosehide Lake. The Junction was so small it had no stop signs and only four fire hydrants. Acting Fire Chief Joe Snell headed up the volunteer department tucked in on a side street just a block from the lake's shore.

Nell Parker's General Store and Post Office, located on the edge of Porcupine Junction, looked out upon mist-shrouded Moosehide Lake. A stranger from down south might refer to Nell's place as a convenience store, but she considered it to be an essential one, not just there to serve the whim or convenience of town's-folk and visitors. Nell stocked such essential healthy products as locally grown vegetables, plus beef and pasteurized milk provided by nearby farmer Frank Sattachi. Nell's own freshly baked products included bread, buns, tarts and muffins. The demand for her scrumptious wild-blueberry pies was so fierce, you were out of luck to buy one unless you got in line before sunrise on her baking days.

Nell Parker was a stocky five foot-two dynamo easily recognized by the white apron usually snuggled around her ample middle. Her chosen dove white apparel hid puffs of flour which inadvertently drifted off her baking frenzies. Smudges of flour however often decorated the tip of her nose or forehead as a result of her baking ventures.

Nell always wore her hair in a tightly rolled bun kept in check by strategically placed pins. She took care that no loose strands of her locks would ever find their way into her baked goods.

Nell's apron was a multi-use piece of apparel. Its spacious front pocket housed wooden spoons and a battery of other implements which were integral to her baking tasks. Her apron was just the ticket for wiping a runny nose or flour covered hands and it kept smudges of grease and smears off her everyday long sleeved dresses. A catchall for crumbs, usually a day never passed without a host of her aprons flapping out to dry on her clothesline. Nell's supply of locally created aprons kept her wardrobe pristine for longer than one would expect.

Bert Parker, Nell's sidekick, was slightly shorter than his wife. In culinary terms, Bert was the salt of their relationship while Nell was the pepper. Nell's dynamic activities were offset by what she referred to as her mate's glacial speed while completing any task on which he had embarked.

Bert never raced to complete any of his projects and he was forever reminding Nell, "Don't forget about that story of the tortoise and the hare, dear."

She usually responded with, "At the rate you get things done, the hare will be dead from old age after waiting for you at the finish line!"

Besides being methodical in his work habits, the same was reflected in Bert's manner of dress. His shoes were seldom scruffy, trousers neatly pressed and his billowing shirt sleeves were kept neatly restrained by an expansion band circumventing his arms just above each elbow.

Bert always carried a fountain pen and mechanical pencil in his shirt pockets. His writing was an extension of his other methodical habits. Whenever Bert wrote a letter such as i or j, he would not simply dot the letter, but place a tiny circle in its place.

Before he embarked on a task for which he was not properly clothed, Nell's husband would don a pair of striped overalls and a cap, both similar to those worn by railroad engineers. His tools were always ready for use, well-oiled, sharpened and handy in his wooden toolbox, which he'd constructed himself.

Folks who dropped by to pick up their mail were Nell's regular and most important customers. Inside her store, next to the post office wicket, there was an overstuffed easy chair, enticing customers to plunk themselves down and enjoy the latest copy of *The Raven Lake Suppository News*, the local scandal sheet of the North. After browsing through the *News*, they could then read the letter they'd received from their Aunt Florence, describing the ladies group's latest bus excursion to Casino Rama, and how she made out shooting craps and playing stud poker at Rama during the trip. Upon request, Nell would serve her customers, sandwiches layered between grand slices of her own bread, accompanied by steaming mugs of her 'Always Fresh Java.'

Hardware items occupied at least half of Nell's establishment. You could find water pump gaskets, wire cutters, pocket watches, pick axes and every imaginable item that you'd expect to find in an old-fashioned hardware emporium dating back before the 1940's. Nell's husband, Bert, rode herd on this end of the business, which included a pair of White Rose gas pumps out front, standing tall and majestic, looking down on stacks of cans of motor oil and jugs of windshield washer fluid. If you snooped through Bert's offerings you might find fishing plugs next to sinkers and perhaps a stock of coal-oil lamps along with a supply of their wicks and fuel, and even an extra-large pair of red long-johns awaiting the next blustering winter. The Parkers placed more faith in stuff from the good old days when there were fewer useless technological gadgets around to supposedly make life easier.

At the extreme end of the spit extending into Moosehide from the shore near Nell's place, Gary Caboose's Big Canoe Marina stuck to the last semblance of dry land like a blister on a moose's behind. A visitor to The Junction might assume the ratty-looking marina building was just a relic left unscorched after the great fire of '29. Further scrutiny would disclose, however, that the derelict structure was actually a hive of activity.

Gary Caboose shared the austere marina building with his missus, Yellow Feather, and their two little Cabooses: Helen, a tiny lass with coal black pigtails, who would only answer to the name 'Little Raven,' and Charles, her porky young brother with red hair and freckles who preferred to be called 'Chuckie.'

Gary's Algonquin genes were a combined mish-mash from an Irish father and a French-Canadian mother, while Yellow Feather's Metis inheritance was a mixture of Iroquois and Scottish. Yellow Feather was a sprightly lass who possessed her own hidden talents. She has been known to gut a trout with amazing speed and dexterity. It paid not to get within range of her flashing fillet knife when she was at work on such a task.

Gary Caboose's arrival upon God's green earth took place on the Algonquin Moose Antler Reserve, within shouting distance of the Junction's fire station, but back in the bush. Gary was lean and lanky, his physique having been honed from hours of canoeing on Moosehide Lake. To boot, his complexion was weathered to the texture of tree bark.

Since there was no school in the Junction, the Caboose kids had to be bussed to a font of higher learning in Raven Lake, a good half hour's trek by snowshoes in the winter whenever bus driver Clyde Wopper slept in.

The remainder of the hamlet's locals was made up of a few dozen odd Porcupiners, whose abodes were sprinkled hither and yon along the Junction's trio of dusty streets, none of which they could afford to pave.

I almost forgot to mention that a series of five roads radiated out from the hamlet like fingers on an arthritic hand. These so-called roads were more like tracks defined by the path of an inebriated moose staggering its way home through the pine, spruce, and birch. Along these trails, homesteaders had created farms by hacking down the bush on land with several acres of good fertile soil in the space left not already taken over by huge granite boulders.

During the blueberry and moose-hunting seasons, the hamlet's businesses boomed. If visitors to the district didn't bring a tent or sleeping bag with them, and wished to hang around until their luck changed, they might be supplied with bed and board at one of the farms in the outback where a hindquarter of moose or four quarts of blueberries would get you two nights lodging if you didn't have the cash.

Gary Caboose rented canoes and aluminum rowboats to would-be fishermen and conducted fly-fishing lessons as he expounded on the virtues of his colourful hand-tied trout flies (the best in the North). As well, he offered excursions on Moosehide Lake for those who didn't know where the largest lunkers lurked.

So those are Porcupine Junction's highlights in a nutshell. If you want anything more exciting than the region has to offer, you'd have to head south to one of the big cities. By doing so however, you'd be leaving behind the peace and quiet of loon country, along with the smell of cedars and smoky campfires.

Considering all it had to offer, Porcupine Junction was the ideal locale for anyone wishing to idle away their idle time, and experience life as it should be lived.

But the winds of change were about to drift out of the wilderness and gust in to disrupt the lives of these contented folks.

2

Bert's FiX-It SHop

For every complex question,
there's always a simple answer
—and it's usually wrong!
(Bert Parker)

A casual observer might say, "Bert's Fix-It Shop is just a haven for lazy old deadbeats," but looks can be deceiving.

To build this shop, a weird structure which had sprouted from his fertile imagination, Bert Parker had fastened a usta-be chicken coop to the side of a derelict drive shed. The aforementioned hens' house sagged against the drive shed as if searching for a convenient spot to collapse from exhaustion or old age.

Located conveniently just outside the back entrance to Nell's General Store and Post Office, Bert had created his shop from these relics of a bygone era, moulding them into what he considered to be a state-of-the-art work area. He had patiently resuscitated the buildings by hammering spikes into any loose dried-out boards, and nailed flattened Campbell Soup cans over knot holes and cracks to thwart unwanted breezes and prying eyes.

On an oak slab, Bert had gouged in calligraphy, letters alerting everyone to the existence of 'Bert's Fix-It Shop.' The letters, a trickle of blood-red enamel flowing into one another, stood out from its surrounding oak grain which was clearly visible through many coats of spar varnish. This signature work of art hung from two horse shoes dangling above the shop's double door entranceway. The metal horse shoes were the ones that Bert had removed from May and Martha, farmer Frank Sattachi's Clydesdale mares after Bert had shod them last year.

The shop was like no other. In broad strokes of charcoal-black lettering, Bert had slapped his credo clearly visible on the wall near the top just inside the main entrance. "If It's Been Made, And It's Broke, We Kin Fix It!"

Samples of every tool ever created by humankind:wrenches, screwdrivers, hammers, pliers, on and on, ad nauseam, all graduated by size from the smallest to the gargantuan, lined the walls. One would certainly expect to find tools inside a repair shop, but not Bert's unusual furnishings.

Scattered around the inside walls was a collection of seating as if there had been an explosion in a Goodwill furniture store. Included was an overstuffed pillow-back recliner next to a bulging leather covered love seat, a stately wing back chair, several kitchen chairs, three rocking chairs and a living room sofa. In total, there were enough seats to accommodate the members of a symphony orchestra. Nell thought that Bert's work space reminded her of a hospital operating theatre, but Myrtle Butler, Nell's twin sister thought it was closer to resembling a Spanish arena, considering the amount of bull she'd heard on the premises from the hangers-on over the years.

Off in the chicken-coop annex of Bert's complex was a sink supplying sparkling drinking water from Bert's crystal spring-fed well, still accessible by a hand operated pump. An electric kettle and coffee pot rested on a counter adjacent to the sink. Fixings for Nell's Finest Java and a can of Tetley teabags were at hand on a shelf above the coffee pot and kettle. A Brown Betty crockery teapot sat beside a well-stocked cookie jar large enough to appease the appetites of even the most ravenous visitors.

Since Bert believed in the wisdom of the

world's other great thinkers, he had mounted a blackboard on the left wall just inside the front entranceway. With a chunk of chalk found on the ledge attached beneath the board, visitors could inscribe on the surface any quotation of their choosing. It might be: *"Age is not important, unless you are a piece of cheese,"* or *"Remember, silence is sometimes the best answer."* The only criteria for any quotation was that it be legible and thought provoking.

Within easy reach of the seating were bookcases with copies of the *Raven Lake Suppository News*, various farm magazines, *The Farmer's Almanac* and a broad assortment of books. This collection of reading material would be the envy of any university library. Scanning through the volumes, I noted a collection of works by Ernest Hemingway, a dozen by author Farley Mowat beside volumes by Marshall McLuhan which included, *The Gutenberg Galaxy* and *Understanding Media*. Volumes of *A History Of The English Speaking Peoples* by Winston Churchill accompanied a set of *Thinking Skills* books by Edward de Bono, the originator of *Lateral Thinking*. Visitors to the shop could borrow at will or add to any of the books. How could such a comfortable setting not attract every manner of character able to reach the site by shank's mare, pedal power, or any bizarre form of locomotion?

Characters who frequented Bert's shop included Clyde Wopper whose beastly yellow International school bus had just rolled to a stop near the main entrance of Bert's hideaway. Clyde slid off the driver's seat of his yellow conveyance and waddled towards the side entrance of Bert's shop. Clyde usually stopped here after he'd dropped off his load of hell raisers at Raven Lake Public school.He'd had a substantial breakfast this day before setting out on his bus route, but his ample paunch still had room for a couple of Nell's macaroons and two or three oatmeal and raisin cookies that he knew he could find in the cookie jar inside. A mug of 'Nell's Always Fresh' java would also hit the spot to wash down his anticipated snack.

Clyde had the build of a chock-full sack of P.E.I. spuds, and his backside, enlarged by hours parked behind the wheel of his coach, protruded aft, giving Clyde a list to starboard when he wandered from point to point. Three lonesome reddish hairs popped up from the centre of his otherwise bald dome. Clyde's lack of cranial foliage was partially offset by a matching bushy moustache resembling the business end of a well-worn floor mop. He was not formally schooled, but possessed a wisdom honed by years of trying to outwit the youngsters he ferried to Raven Lake School and on trips to museums, farms and other supposed points of educational interest. Although not formally well educated, Clyde would have to be considered to be one of those individuals classified in the vernacular as 'street smart.'

Clyde knew that Bert usually unlocked his shop doors at sunrise each day, but he was surprised on this occasion to find four others already waiting inside. Clyde moseyed up to the blackboard inside the shop, picked up a stick of chalk, and in his own inimitable scrawl wrote, *"Good judgement comes from experience, and a lot of that comes from bad judgement."* He then headed for his favourite rocking chair next to Abner Moss, sitting stately as usual in his favourite wing-back chair. Abner's long face and protruding jaw reminded Clyde of an orangutan, and the lenses of Abner's gold rimmed spectacles looked as though they might have been cut from a plate glass window. His prominent bifocals had earned Abner Moss the obvious nickname of 'Specs.'

Pointing to the quotation that Clyde had just written on the blackboard, Abner remarked, "You know a lot about bad judgement, don't you, Clyde?"

To which Clyde merely replied, "How else do you think I got to be so much smarter than you?" Clyde wandered over to the bookcase and tucked three mystery books by Agatha Christie wherever there was space in amongst the other volumes. "Here are some books worth reading Abner. I can help you with the big words if you like."

Howard Oakley, Jim O'Connor and Abner Moss sat in a row. Jim, in the middle of the three, was parked on the end of a leather-topped love seat, his left leg dangling over the loveseat's arm leaving his size ten work boot free to hoof Abner's chair if he thought 'Specs' wasn't paying attention to the latest arguments. Howard Oakley sat perched on the far left of the group on an over-stuffed pillow recliner. Room remained on Jimmy's loveseat for Ralph Schmidt to park his carcass on the fraction that Big Jim had left unoccupied.

Arriving in Canada as a German immigrant before retiring to Porcupine Junction, Ralph Schmidt had been brew master for a Southern Ontario microbrewery in Creemore. His auburn locks were usually slicked back with Brylcream into a tiny ducktail. Ralph always found ample time to brew his own brand of a dark British stout as a hobby and 'Suds' Schmidt could easily be convinced to bring in a few bottles of his latest elixir for the boys to sample.

Even though the 'Krauts' had lost the Second World War to the 'Limies,' Ralph still preferred a strong British brew to the less robust brands brewed in his Fatherland. When it came to matters of satisfying his thirst and enjoying British beer, Ralph forgot about losing the Second World War, preferring to let bygones be bygones.

Ignoring his favourite rocking chair, Clyde headed towards the space where he would be able to squeeze his bulk in on the loveseat between Big Jim and Ralph.

This collection of characters which usually hung around Bert's shop was always ready to propose solutions to the world's problems and offer Bert advice on repairs to contraptions on which he was at the time working.

Nell stepped out onto her back porch and with furrowed brow headed towards Bert's hideaway. She yanked open the door and roared, "Are you in there Bert?"

"Yes, dear. I just finished sharpening the blades on Mildred's push mower an' I'm patching Rufus McCoy's flat bicycle tire."

"We've got a problem, Bert! I'm sick and tired of your cronies parading through my kitchen on their way to using our toilet! Besides, our septic system can't keep up much longer with the volume of crap it has to process from them. Your brain trust out here is going to have to come up with a solution to this problem within the next couple of days."

"I'll check with the lads today, Nell, to see if we can resolve your dilemma."

Bert returned to his work repairing the tube and replacing the bicycle tire back onto its rim. As soon as he finished, he turned to those present. "You heard her boys. Any suggestions?"

Big Jimmy O'Connor was the first to come up with an idea. "I assume the solution has to be quick, cheap and environmentally friendly? What you need Bert is an outhouse located not far from your shop."

"We can't build a privy in just a couple of days, Jim."

In response to Bert's concern, Big Jim continued. "Frank Sattachi's got one that's standin' out by his barn. I'm sure he'd be willing to part with it. All we need to do is find a suitable spot near here, dig a pit, then move Frank's outhouse over."

Bert pulled on his left ear lobe and rubbed the side of his nostril as he considered the suggestion, "Finding a spot to park the outhouse will be no problem. There's a great site over there behind them trees, but how are we going to get Frank's privy over here?"

It was time for Clyde Wopper to wade in on the problem. "I've got a hitch on the back of my coach, and Bert and I know Frank's got a trailer. I've borrowed it before."

Bert smiled at the prospect. "Sounds good to me. The spot out of sight over there is not too close to my well so there'd be no chance of polluting our drinking water."

Bert left the job of ~~connecting~~ contacting Frank Sattachi with Clyde Wopper, and placed Big Jim O'Connor in charge of arranging a crew to dig the pit and help hoist the privy on and off the trailer.

Frank was glad to get rid of the eyesore and

readily loaned the group the use of his trailer. His front end loader came in handy to get the building onto the trailer before the group changed its mind. As the flotilla passed through the streets of the Junction The sight of the outhouse perched on the trailer behind the yellow school bus caused a bit of a stir. In response to the questions from local citizens as to what he was up to, Clyde Wopper, with a straight face, replied, "We're getting our float ready for Porcupine Junction's entry in next year's Raven Lake Fall Fair parade."

Within one day, the task had been completed and the new facility was fully operational. Big Jim asked Bert, "What do you think Nell will say when she gets wind of our solution?"

"I'll just tell her how cheaply we solved the problem and assure her the breezes seldom blow from the outhouse's direction down towards her kitchen and clothesline."

"I've got one more small job for you Jim,. Would you whip up a couple of book shelves for inside the new crapper? I've got several books of political cartoons and an old Eaton's catalogue that I was going to bring in. We might as well store them in the outhouse for a bit of light reading."

Stormy Weather Surprise

Gary Caboose stepped gingerly off the dock and into his favourite cedar-strip canoe. His son Charles 'Chuckie' caboose and his daughter Helen followed reluctantly in their father's footsteps. As the two kids hunkered down in a comfortable spot on the one remaining empty seat, Gary paddled away from the Big Canoe Marina dock.

The sun had not yet climbed over the horizon and the usual morning mists hung like a giant puff of milkweed just above Moosehide's choppy waters. As Gary dug in his paddle, the bow of the craft sliced through the eddies leaving a trail of bubbles in its wake. Gary was heading into familiar waters, but the questionable weather would determine his itinerary for the remainder of the day.

Chuckie was the first to express his displeasure. "I don't like the looks of them clouds. Why couldn't I have stayed home to check on my rabbit snares?"

Gary's methodical stroke didn't miss a beat. "You can check your traps over when we get back. Don't worry, a little rain won't do you any harm and we've ridden out storms before."

There was method in Gary's early-morning madness. Last evening he had completed tying his latest fishing fly which he had christened the Muskaboomer. This was not just another of Gary's superlative fishing flies. It was to be the ultimate weapon in his arsenal intended to entice a massive Muskie lurking hidden along Moosehide's shores.

Gary could barely contain his determination to test the newest creation among his unique and carefully-tied fishing flies. To increase the lure's potential, Gary called upon the skills of Isaac Quail Tail, the reserves medicine man to cast a spell upon the new fly to cloak it with irresistible powers of attraction.

Isaac had built a smoky fire from dried bulrushes, tossed in a pair of beaver claws, a handful of scales from a Big-Mouth Bass and a tuft of otter fur. He chanted a series of mysterious incantations into the swirling smoke, all intended to hoodwink the elusive Muskie into striking the lure.

Gary's prime objective on the outing with his youngsters was to display his superior fishing skills to his two children while testing the attractive powers of his new lure.

Chuckie and Little Raven were not as enthusiastic about the expedition as their father. Helen moaned, "When will we get there? These bugs are eating me alive."

Gary didn't worry about the complaints. The head wind was soon stiffening, after which the insects would be kept in check. "Cast one of your flies. That'll keep you occupied instead of worrying about bugs."

What had begun as what Gary hoped would be a sunny day was now turning out to be a rough stormy one. The mist thickened to a dense black cloud which settled like a shroud over the vessel and its occupants.

Gary knew that he would soon be near the spot where his quarry would probably be lurking in the shallows (particularly in weather like this). There was a sudden flash of lightening followed by a rumble of thunder through the low scudding clouds. When the lightning flashed, Gary's arm was poised to begin a cast which he instinctively completed. His eyes had been trained on a spot between a partly submerged log and a granite boulder. He was sure that he'd seen a ripple in the weeds just as he was completing his cast. When the lure struck the water, the surface exploded and Gary's line snapped taunt. It took both hands on his fly rod to keep it from being torn from his grip. He could feel the canoe being dragged through the waters into a channel feeding into Moosehide Lake. He could do nothing but cling tightly to the rod. Gary could see the back and top fin of the Muskie as the monster looped around through the shallows in a figure eight. The magnificent giant leapt into the air, shook its head, spit out Gary's lure then disappeared into the depths of Moosehide.

Gary's hopes for a successful catch vanished as his line went slack, but he now had a new problem to contend with as the canoe ground to a halt on a sand bar. The falling rain increased in intensity as the group clambered ashore looking for shelter. Fortunately, they quickly discovered a cave in the rock face. Just inside the deep depression's entrance, Gary gathered dry twigs and branches to create a fire, and barbeque the trout that Helen had hauled in, while Charles found a blueberry bush just outside the shelter's entrance. Chuckie's hatful of berries was a welcome addition to the barbequed catch.

Even though they were forced to spend the night in the bush, Gary concluded the expedition turned out positively in the long run. He was now convinced that his new Muskie lure did the job for which it was intended.

The following day after the storm had lost its fury, the family fished on their return trip home. They all hauled in their share of the catch with the result that by the time they arrived back at the marina, they had one pike, six Big-Mouth Bass, three trout and two Pickerel. Little Raven made sure that her mother knew that her trout was the largest catch of the day. All in all, there were enough fish to keep Yellow Feather's flashing filet knife busy, and provided the family with tasty fish dinners to the end of following week.

3

The Moose Hunters

Don't count your years,
Make your years count.
(Jack Spratt)

Jack Spratt and Clifford Benham were moose hunters from down south of Porcupine Junction. Due to his diminished stature, Jack was often addressed as 'Shorty,' while Cliff's more bearish size earned him the nickname 'Grizzly.'

One fine fall day during the moose–hunting season, the two so-called hunters headed for Porcupine County after having purchased the appropriate hunting licences. They didn't expect it would take them long to bag a magnificent male moose with a fine set of antlers. In fact, Jack had more-or-less promised his girlfriend Lucinda an impressive rack of moose antlers for her to present to her father.

'Shorty' an' 'Grizzly' set out in Jack's beat-up Chevy pickup and spent a full day scouting around Porcupine County where there were plenty of signs, but the pair had no actual sightings of moose. They were getting exasperated and time was running out with no kills.

Late in the afternoon of that first day, they navigated along a gravelled pothole infested bush road, when they came to a small clearing where Cliff spotted a log cabin amongst the trees.

"Hang on a minute, Shorty. Pull in over there near that cabin." When they got closer, he said, It looks abandoned. Maybe we could bunk there for the night. We haven't got any extra cash for accommodation and I'd kinda' like to hang around for one more day to see if our luck will change."

Jack thought that sounded like a good idea (besides he was still thinking about the rack of moose antlers that he'd return with for his girlfriend's father). "Sounds good to me. Let's go and have a look through the window to see if the place is inhabited."

They stepped down from the cab of the Chevy and headed towards the cabin. They could see that some of the caulking had fallen out between several of the logs, but in general, the cabin seemed to be in reasonable condition.

Jack used his sleeve to wipe a clear spot on the cabin's dirty window. Peering inside they could see a stone fireplace on one wall along one end of the cabin and a wooden bunk bed nailed to the end wall opposite the fireplace. There was what looked to be a rickety table with one chair and a stool in the middle of the floor. A door on one end of the room appeared to be nailed shut but there was a chewed-out hole at the bottom of the door, probably gnawed through by a beaver or porcupine.

With a squeal from the rusty hinges, Cliff pushed the cabin's door until it was completely open. Then he stepped inside. There was a scurrying sound from behind the door, and a porcupine scuttled across the floor and out through the chewed opening in the bottom of the nailed-shut end door.

There was a dirty mattress on the bottom bunk, but only boards on the top bed. "It sure looks abandoned to me," Cliff said, "especially considering the thick layer of dust on everything. I could crash out on the bottom bunk mattress, an' we could bring in the blanket from your Chevy's seat. With that and your jacket you'd be nice an' snug up on the top."

"You're right, Grizz. There's no reason we couldn't camp here for the night. I noticed a lot of moose droppings in the area so we should be able to bag what we're here for in the morning."

"Actually I believe some of that scat is from bear, but I think you're right. This looks like a good place to hang our hats for the night." Cliff threw his coat onto the back of the chair and flopped onto the mattress. A cloud of dust erupted and after a quick rustle, three field mice popped through a hole in the mattress at the foot of the bed. The tiny critters scurried down the leg of the bed, scuttled across the floor and disappeared through the chewed out opening in the bottom of the door.

"Well Cliff, this place may be abandoned, but it sure ain't empty!"

Cliff rolled over on the mattress. "Toss me my jacket will you?" He rolled it up as a pillow and tucked it under his head.

"You look like you're set there for the rest of the night."

"Nope, but I am getting jest a shade hungry. Why don't you go out an' bring in them two burgers we bought in Raven Lake. They'll have to do until morning."

A few minutes later Jack returned from the pickup with the seat blanket over his arm and clutching a paper bag containing the two burgers.

"It's a bit cool in here," said Cliff. "I wonder if that fireplace works?"

"Well, there's one way to find out. " Jack used his jacket to dust off the table then sat down the bag of burgers. "I'll go out an' get some dry twigs and a bit of whatever larger stuff I can find. You check in my jacket pocket for a book of matches."

Cliff rolled off the bunk from his comfy position and rummaged through the pockets of Shorty's jacket until he located the book of matches.

A short while later, Jack entered with an armful of small branches and pieces of wood.

"We're in luck,"Cliff said. "I found your matches."

Jack arranged a pile of twigs in the fireplace and placed a few larger chunks of the driest wood on top. It didn't take them long to ignite. The first flash of flame from the burning twigs licked up onto the topmost layer of larger branches. However, it wasn't long before smoke from their efforts began to billow out from the fireplace and into the room. The ersatz hunters heard a scrambling up the chimney. Leaves and twigs fell down from the opening and the falling debris burst into flame, adding to the smoke.

Jack popped out through the cabin doorway and looked up onto the roof towards the stone chimney. A cluster of squirrels were scrambling out through the flue and across the roof. Just the odd hint of smoke was escaping from the flue itself.

Using the door as a fan Cliff attempted to draw some of the smoke out of the cabin. The rusty hinges squealed in protest as he worked the door back and forth.

Jack hollered from outside, "Come on out an' give me a boost onto the roof. I'll grab a branch an' jam it down the flue to see if I can't get rid of that bloody squirrels' nest that must be pluggin' up the chimney."

Cliff hoisted Jack onto the roof and when he got to the chimney, he poked away at the top of the chimney opening, trying to clear the flue. As he dug into the flue with a branch a sudden belch of smoke puffed out of the chimney like a steam engine's smoke erupting from under a trestle as the train passed through. The blast of smoke knocked Jack onto his arse on the roof.

Down below, Cliff was trying to get rid of more smoke, by waving and fanning his jacket near the open front door.

Shorty shouted down, "I think we got her now Cliff. Most of that smoke should soon get sucked out. Gimme a hand down off this roof. I don't want to break my neck after all this!"

When they were both back inside and the clouds of smoke had thinned out, Cliff plopped onto the rickety chair and Jack parked his backside onto the stool. They spent the next few minutes congratulating themselves on their latest success, and polished off the two burgers.

By this time, it was getting dark. The smoke

was more or less cleared from the cabin, and the chill was off the air. Jack lugged in a few more dry chunks of wood to last them during the night and piled the supply near the fire place. Cliff gave Jack a boost into the top bunk, but 'Grizzly' had one more job before he settled down for the night. He lumbered out to the pickup and returned with his double-barreled twelve gauge shotgun.

Jack watched from the top bunk as Cliff loaded and cocked both barrels. "What are doing with that cannon?"

"There's bears around here you know. I'll just stand it up here in the corner in case of an emergency during the night."

"Ain't that a bit dangerous to leave a loaded weapon like that around?"

"Naw, it'll be okay. I won't forget it's here. Go to sleep."

On that reassuring note, they were soon both snoring contentedly after the day's exertions. The blaze in the fireplace gradually winked out, but by then the inside of the cabin was comfy and warm.

At about four in the morning, Cliff's bladder told him it was in need of relief. It was as dark as the inside of a coal-miner's nostrils as he stumbled through the doorway. Just as he finished unzipping his trousers, he heard a deep rumbling growl. Without taking time to finish what he'd gone out for, he was back inside considerably quicker than he'd gone out.

In his rush to get back into the lower bunk, he knocked over the rickety chair, which fell against the loaded shotgun standing against the wall. This chain of events led to the shotgun discharging both barrels. The first blast blew a second hole in the nailed-shut side door. When the second barrel went off, it cleaned out most of the glass in the cabin's only window.

Jack in the upper bunk sprung to life as if he'd been jabbed by a cattle prod. "What the Hell was that!"

"Go back to sleep, Jack."

"That's easy for you to say."

"I was just scarin' off a bear that was lurking around outside the cabin. I'm sure he's gone now."

In spite of the shotgun incident, they were both eventually snoring again. Cliff remained crashed out until birds singing brought him to life again. In addition to the birds, Cliff became aware of a scuffling sound on the floor. He peered over the edge of his bunk and discovered that the mysterious noise originated from the region of the gnawed out hole at the bottom of the nailed-shut second door. What he witnessed was the parade of a family of skunks. Momma skunk out in front followed by four youngsters with the head of the household bringing up the rear.

The group headed directly for the bunk-beds, and settled down underneath where he was lying. His mind raced as to how he could get out of bed and the cabin without disturbing the critters.

It was then that a whisper came from above, "Pssst, Cliff, are you awake?"

"Shhhh!"

"What do you mean, 'Shhh'?"

"Just what I said. We've got a family of skunks under our bed."

" WAADYA MEAN?"

"For God's sake, quiet down. I mean real skunks under my bed. We've gotta figger a way to get outta here without creatin' a stink."

Jack puzzled over the problem for a moment then whispered, "Okay, this is what we'll do, I'll count to three, an' as soon as I hit three, I'll bail out of here and head for the door. Then you foller me as quick as you can."

"Okay, since you're first man out, don't ferget that door is latched. You better get it open real quick. You don't know how fast I can move, 'specially in a case like this!"

"Okay let's get goin' or we'll never get out of here."

On the count of three Jack rolled out of the top bunk. He landed running, but stumbled when he got to the door. Cliff was right behind him and scooped him off the floor as they both fumbled to open the latch. Cliff's exit from the bottom bunk had not been graceful, but there are no marks for form in an emergency like this. It is surprising how fast a big man can move when he has to!

Once outside, they congratulated each other over their escape from near disaster. Jack turned to Cliff. "You know this cabin was supposed to be abandoned, but I think since we've arrived, every critter in Porcupine County has decided to pay it a visit. I suggest we spend the rest of the day huntin'. I've got a feelin' our string of bad luck is about to run out."

"Okay, them skunks are probably gone by now, but if we got nuthin' by noon I'm outta' here, moose, or no moose."

The unlucky hunters checked out the area for miles around the cabin but encountered no moose.

Since their allotted time had almost run its course, Jack suggested one final and desperate move. "We got no moose, and I hate to go home empty-handed, but we've passed all kinds of blueberry bushes during our rambling. I've got several tins in the back of the truck. I must have been psychic tossin' them cans in the back. Let's pick as many berries as we can. At least we won't go home empty handed.

The pair sweated for three and a half hours, and in the end managed to gather four pails filled to the brim. To sum up their hunting expedition, Cliff asked, "What are you going to tell your girlfriend about the moose antlers that you never got to bring back for her father?"

"I'll think up some cock-an'-bull story to tell her about how you rescued me from the jaws of a charging black bear. I'll tell her she should be thankful that I made it back alive. Then I'll give the blueberries to my aunt and she can make a couple of pies for us, but I needn't tell Lucinda about them, or she might get suspicious of my story."

As Jack and Cliff were departing from the area in Jack's battered Chevy, if they'd bothered to look back at the abandoned cabin, they might have noticed the huge animal with a magnificent set of antlers as the beast stood next to the glassless cabin window.

The bull-moose poked its snout in through the opening, sniffed twice, and meandered off into the bush.

4

A Village Comes To Life

Do not seek to follow
in the footsteps of men of old:
seek what they sought.
(Abner Moss)

Each morning as the sun inched its way over the horizon, Nell meandered out onto her general store's front porch. She would settle into her rocking chair and gaze out upon the mists hovering over Moosehide Lake. Nell never ceased to be amazed at the display of morning brilliance as slivers of the sun's rays sought to penetrate through the haze. Colours ranged through all variations of the spectrum: scintillating oranges, scarlet and even hints of pink and violet. No morning was ever the same as there was always the unexpected from the Almighty's palette of brilliant hues. This was Nell's own personal time when she would contemplate decisions in her life, and muse over what might be in store for her in the days ahead.

On these early morning periods of thoughtful relaxation, Nell's usual companion for the past dozen years had been her faithful mutt, Buddy, who now lay flopped on the porch next to two tall baskets of freshly picked apples, a bag of onions and a collection of pumpkins. At first glance, anyone might assume the resident animal was a Golden Labrador. However, if you looked closely, you might spot a hint of the rusty coat Buddy inherited from the Retriever that had contributed to the male half of his parentage. Buddy's paws were the size of dinner plates, and his thick curly coat would have put any self respecting sheep to shame.

As Buddy lay collapsed on the porch, Nell continued to contemplated the sunrise and assumed her companion was likely dreaming about his next meal. Although Buddy was part Retriever, Nell had never seen Old Budd retrieve a thing in his whole life, with the exception of his next meal which he usually wolfed down with lightning speed. If there was anything in life in which Buddy excelled, it would be relaxin' and eatin'. Nell often wondered, with the amount of sleeping he did, how Buddy could always be so hungry. I guess the old hound's snoozing consumed more calories than even she realized.

The breezes were fresh and the sounds of birdlife comforting. The soaring gulls and the intermittent mating calls of a pair of loons penetrated the morning serenity. Nell thought back to the time she'd first stood on the shore of Moosehide Lake.

In the 1800's her grandfather, John James Hurley, had purchased fifty acres of prime land for forty dollars from the local Indian agent. John James had then constructed a log cabin on the site and cleared much of the bush from the virgin acreage.

However, it wasn't until approximately half a century ago that Nell had first stood on Moosehide's shore with her own father, Bill Hurley, looking out over the misty lake. The log cabin had long since vanished into the mists of time as had her grandfather.

There were a baker's dozen brothers and sisters in her immediate family, and Nell was the youngest. She had made the trek to Saskatoon to begin her career as a secretary, but felt compelled to return to the family farm when her mother died. When she returned home from the west, Nell ran the household for her aging father until he eventually passed away.

In his younger days, William Hurley was known as 'Big Bill' Hurley. He had a massive girth plus the strength of several men and it was a longstanding family joke that the distance around Bill's neck was equal to the distance around his wife Matilda's waist. There were reports that when helping to construct a neighbour's barn, Bill could lift one end of a barn beam by himself. As an additional display of his strength, neighbours would often see Bill carrying his supplies. He'd have a hundredweight of grain tucked under one arm, an equivalent weight of flour under the other and hoisting a fifty pound bag of sugar in one hand.

When it came to settling disputes between either friends or foe, Bill could do so by brute strength but he much preferred to use wisdom or negotiation. He was an expert in the practice of 'looming.' If there was ever a dispute, Bill's looming presence was enough to ward off any attempt to challenge his strength. Bill Hurley's feats of strength and his reputation for fairness made him a character recognized by every resident of Algoma.

By the time Bill died, Nell's brothers and sisters had already left the farm to pursue independent lives. Consequently, Nell's father bequeathed the fifty lakeside acres on the shore of Moosehide to Nell.

Her siblings shared the inheritance of the two hundred other acres of the family farm south of Moosehide Lake, but Nell always felt that her fifty acre inheritance was the best part of the settlement. She valued that property as much as her grandfather and father did when they were alive and in their memory she was determined to see that her tiny piece of heaven was always treated with the utmost respect.

Following Bill Hurley's death, Nell returned to Saskatoon where she met Bert Parker. They were married out west and returned to the shore of Moosehide where Bert built the structure which eventually evolved into Nell's General Store and Post Office.

Nell could best be described as stocky but sprightly. She was not the most diplomatic. In fact, Bert described his mate as being a graduate of the 'Attila the Hun School of Diplomacy.' Nell's idea of getting a person's attention was to whack them between the eyes with a two by four. Even though she could be abrupt, she was more often than not right.

In contrast to Nell's peppery conduct, Bert was

a short neat considerate gentleman considered by many to be the salt of the earth. As I previously mentioned, his aim when completing a task was to be thorough and precise, but not necessarily speedy. Bert and Nell Parker shared similar objectives in life. They were both hardworking honest folks who believed in being self-sufficient. They had faith in the past and were not ones to buy into promises of the modern world of technology. They were not averse to progress, but felt that they should be able to pick and choose the best of what was offered in the field of innovations.

As Nell continued day-dreaming on the porch, she was entranced with Nature's panorama. It was at this point in her reverie that she became conscious of one of her faithful hound's less admirable traits. On occasion, trying to satisfy his insatiable appetite, Buddy would devour flotsam along the shores of Moosehide. It might be a long expired gull, a rotting bass, or a raccoon or other deceased critter from back of the woods. The consumption of such delicacies would challenge Buddy's digestive system, causing it to emit an odour which Nell had long ago learned to recognize. What she'd just experienced was one more such occasion.

"Phew, Buddy! You sure know how to clean out a person's nasal passages. I'm heading back to the shop until the air clears around here." Nell hoofed through the doorway into the store and headed back towards Bert's shop. She found her husband puttering with what looked like the drive shaft of a Model A Ford roadster that he was rebuilding. "You remember what we were talking about last night, Bert. I've decided to go ahead with all three businesses."

The dozen odd characters sitting around watching, responded with quizzical looks.

"Perhaps you'd better explain," said Bert. "I'll have to clarify your remark to this crowd later anyway."

Nell figured she might as well do as Bert suggested. "As you all likely know, since I inherited these fifty acres, I've sold off a few lots for houses, and a chunk of land for the fire hall. Years ago a lumber Barron, Klaus Barnaby, approached me seeking to buy up my fifty acre town site. He promised me top dollar for it, but I wouldn't sell the land to him because I wanted to keep the Junction just as it was. He said I was nuts because I could make a lot of money on the deal."

A couple of heads nodded in agreement and Nell continued. "Cash is important, but in my books it isn't as important as preserving the way of life we have here in the Junction."

More nodding heads joined in as Bert added his own words of advice. "She's right, you know!"

Nell had more to say. "We have a grand little place here and I think my dad and grand dad would have wanted me to keep it that way."

A few faces looked up expectantly and Nell went on. "But we can't stand in the way of progress forever. Three businessmen have approached me and want to purchase lots next to my store." She held up one finger. "Benedict Hong is Chinese and he wants to open a restaurant." Another finger snapped up. "Then there's Wallace Bottomley. He's British and hopes to operate a drug store, and finally—" Her third finger shot up. "Luigi Silvano, an Italian, who has a barber shop in mind."

"It sounds like the United Nations is movin' in, Nell," piped up a voice from the crowd.

"That might be so, but for a variety of reasons, I think Porcupine Junction will benefit from these three businesses. I talked to all three of these gentlemen and explained what kind of community we have here. I believe they will all fit in fine, but just to make sure, I've asked them all to appear here in Bert' bullpen at one p.m. tomorrow afternoon. They'll explain what they have in mind, and if you have any concerns about their motives, you'll have a chance to pick their brains. Perhaps by the time you've finished with them, they might make an about face and look for greener pastures elsewhere to establish their businesses. Any questions?"

None arose, and with that task complete, Nell headed back to her rocking chair on the store's front porch, hoping that the breezes off Moosehide would have cleared the air by then. Looking down at Buddy, Nell doubted that the old dog had stirred even a single hair since she had left. He continued wheezing, whistling, and snoring, punctuated by the odd grunt as he probably dreamed about chasing a squirrel, chipmunk, or other similar quarry through the bush. "Well Buddy, it will be interesting to see how my three new business prospects make out in the teeth of that lot tomorrow."

Nell decided that she'd place a bowl of dog food on the front porch tomorrow just before one p.m. Hopefully this would keep Buddy occupied while the meeting was taking place in Bert's shop. "I wouldn't want one of your potent emissions being responsible for clearing out tomorrow's meeting before it gets underway."

The next afternoon at exactly one p.m., Bert stood in the centre of his shop where he held a stainless steel milk pail in his left hand, and a lag bolt fitted with two large nuts in his right. He hammered the lag bolt against the pail, giving it three good whacks. "This meeting will now come to order!" The racket would have caught the attention of the most stone deaf, even if their hearing aids had been turned off.

Bert doubted that any person interested in the Junction's welfare was not present for the advertised meeting. He'd even had Big Jim O'Connor lug in a half dozen square bales of straw to provide additional seating for the expected overflow.

The three new business prospects occupied padded kitchen chairs arranged along one side of a well-used oak kitchen table sitting in the centre of Bert's work space. The first to make their pitch was a short Oriental chap on Bert's immediate right. He stood, walked up to the blackboard on the wall, and wrote the following quotation:

'*He who neglects to drink of the spring of experience will die of thirst in the desert of ignorance.*' Then he turned and said, "I heard about Bert's blackboard, so thought I would contribute my own quotation for this occasion. Good afternoon folks, my name is Benedict Hong. You can call me Benedict, Ben, Bonsai-Ben, or Bonsai, or even 'Hey You' if you want to get my attention."

A sense of comfort that settled over the crowd. Bert smiled.

"I gained my experience working as a cook in a lumber camp in British Columbia. A fire devastated the area, so with cash that I'd saved and my severance pay from the destroyed mill, I headed east and would like to set up my own cafe here in Porcupine Junction."

No one spoke and he continued. "My dad worked on the Trans Canada Railway laying track on the original line that used to run through the North back in the 1800's. He immigrated to Canada from Beijing and has long since died. He might even have been one of the labourers who hammered in spikes to anchor that line that once ran past Porcupine Junction."

The gratitude towards his father's struggles was clear from the tone in his voice.

"I plan to call my chow house, *The Golden Phoenix Cafe*, as I expect it to rise from the ashes of my previous work place. I aim to offer the best meals you've ever eaten. My recipes come from years of experience, satisfyin' the hearty appetites of lumberjacks. I served a lot of hungry workers and can claim no instance of food poisoning during all those years to tarnish my reputation. I plan to offer unique meals using local game: rabbit, squirrel, venison, moose, or any other fish or fowl that might appear at my door from local sources.

A few eyebrows went up.

"My meals might be baked, boiled, stewed, barbequed, roasted or fried, but of one thing you can be sure, they will be delicious. Quality meals at fair prices and you'll be able to eat in or take out. I won't force you to use chopsticks, and will even rustle up an egg roll or bowl of won ton soup for those who assume that Chinese food is all I'd be offering."

To emphasize his point, he held up a pair of chopsticks in his right hand. They solidly gripped a knife and fork.

"If you ever have any beef about my food or service being provided, I will personally guarantee your satisfaction. During the buffet I'm providing following this meeting, I'd be happy to answer any of your questions, but I'd better clam up now, and let my other two friends here get their two cents worth in. Don't forget to ask me before you leave though, why I think life is like opening a can of sardines."

Somebody clapped and a few more joined in.

Wallace Bottomley was the next prospect to state his case. Wallace was an impressive man, not quite as relaxed as Ben Hong, but he exuded a good deal of confidence. His square jaw was thrust forward and his neatly groomed silver hair gave him an air of dignity.

"My name is Wallace Bottomley. I'm originally from Bedford, England, and possess a degree in pharmacy from the University of Birmingham. I served as a Regimental Sergeant-Major in the British Army's Lancashire Regiment during the Second World War."

He stopped to let that sink in and then continued. "I'd like to establish a drug store to be called *The Medicine Chest* here in Porcupine Junction. Besides filling prescriptions, my intention is to include a naturopathic section as well. I've already spoken to headman Martin Eagle Claw of the Moose Antler Reserve and he has offered the services of his medicine man to provide native cures for those inclined to try them. I'd also like to offer courses in First Aid and CPR because one never knows when such skills might come in handy here in the wilderness."

That produced several vigourous nods from his audience.

"I have already spoken to Dr. Oliver Doolittle whom some of you might already know. The good doctor is retiring from his practice in Raven Lake, and would like to open an office on the street level here in conjunction with my pharmacy. I'd like to include two apartments above the store, one for my wife and me, and the other for Doctor and Mrs. Doolittle."

He paused again and after clearing his throat went on. "I've heard that most folks in this audience have a hobby, or possess an unusual skill. Mine happens to be knitting. I learned to knit while I was in the British Army, and find it to be a very relaxing hobby. I would be quite happy to share some of my favourite patterns with anyone interested."

A couple of people nodded to each other.

"I see that your boarding house co-owners Hazel McCulloch, Mildred McKay and Myrtle Butler, of 'The Dew Drop Inn' are here today. They expressed an interest in me putting on a knitting clinic at their lodge once I get settled. There might even be closet male knitters here today waiting to be recognized and I'd be happy to offer knitting classes open to male and female alike if I'm not busy with classes in CPR or First Aid."

The three women smiled at each other.

"My experience in the British Army taught me the practice of issuing orders, a skill that my wife has not yet recognized even after ten years of marriage. Perhaps if conditions warrant, I'll have the opportunity to display some of my organizational talents that have gathered a little dust since the Battle of Britain and on that note I'll turn the floor over to the gentleman who hopefully may become your resident tonsorial artist."

The women clapped and the focus of all eyes shifted to Luigi Silvano who wasn't much taller than Bonsai Ben. He'd have to stand on tip toes to trim the locks of some of his taller customers seated in his barber's chair. Luigi was slightly less corpulent than Clyde Wopper and he sported a neatly manicured ebony goatee and matching pencil-thin moustache.

Luigi's gray vest was set off by his white shirt, the sleeves which were held in check by bright red expansion arm-bands just above each elbow. His sombre string tie was fastened in a neat bow and the sharp creases of his dark slacks ended at a pair of polished pointed leather coal black Dacks.

"My shop would be called, *The Clip Joint*. I can't offer you a shave and a haircut for two bits, but I can assure you that after a shave, shampoo or dye job, you'll leave my shop feeling like a million bucks. But in my Clip Joint, I won't be clipping your wallets or purses. My prices will be competitive."

To emphasize his dexterity with the tools of his trade, Luigi held up a straight razor and thumbed the cutting edge.

"I've heard that the residents of the Junction are always interested in learning new stuff, so I thought I'd pass along a brief history of barber poles rather than rave about the topnotch service I intend to offer. During the middle ages, besides cutting hair and shaving whiskers, barbers were responsible for leeching, tooth extraction, and other such procedures and to advertise their services, they'd wrap a bloody bandage around the poles outside of their shops. Now we advertise our barbering businesses by painting red and white stripes around the poles outside our shops. A blue spiral stripe was added later, I suppose just for aesthetic reasons."

He held up the razor he still held. "I use a straight razor, clippers and scissors but assure you that you won't have to seek out the services of Dr. Doolittle or Wallace Bottomley to get patched up after being nicked at my shop."

A half dozen fellows grinned and nodded.

"Besides being a barber, I am a connoisseur of fine wines, many of which I brew myself."

On that note, Luigi put down his razor and fished two wine bottles from a sack bedside his chair.

"I'll leave these two at Ben's buffet for anyone who may wish to sample the results of my latest batch."

That brought bigger smiles from the group and a shifting in chairs.

He went on. "Before I finish, I'd like to pass on another tidbit of tonsorial wisdom. If there are two barbers in a shop, always ask for the one with the poorest haircut." He paused and then said, "He's obviously the one who cut the hair of the one with the better trim."

That got a good laugh.

Since each businessman had said his piece, Bert stood up and said, "You'll have a half hour to chow down on the goodies supplied by Benedict Hong. Then we'll reconvene for questions and that will end the meeting."

A half hour later, the horde had devoured most of the vitals supplied by Bonsai Ben, and Bert called the meeting back to order, using his patented method of hammering on the milk pail.

"I have a few points to clarify and address before we call it a day, but it appears our visitors have gained the confidence of those present. Are there any questions which have not been answered?"

Abner Moss was the first to speak. "I asked Ben Hong why life was like opening a can of sardines and he said, 'because we're all looking for the key.' Well, Bert, I'd like your opinion on what you believe the key is for the residents of Porcupine Junction."

Bert cleared his throat before answering. "As you all know, the world is in a mess. The environment is a shambles, species are disappearing, there is an endless series of wars, greed is rampant, and society has become a slave to technology. With computers, smart phones, television, and a multitude of other gadgets, we are losing the ability to do anything for ourselves. Imagine a car that drives and parks itself! I think the number of new functions on vehicles is probably what's causing so many recalls these days. Advertising and commercialism are smothering our common sense, and our ability to survive has been thrown out through life's window, like an old pair of socks."

He took a big breath after his speech. Then he held up a cell phone. "I bought one of these gismos recently just to see what I was missing. Surely we can get along with our lives nicely without one of these contraptions!"

He shook his head and continued. "I have tried to combat many of these potential problems here in the Junction, but we must remain vigilant to continue on that tact and try to overcome as many as we can. I know that most people in our village have a hobby or some skill at which they excel, whether it's beekeeping, taxidermy, wood carving, storytelling or playing a musical instrument. These are important qualities essential to create a richness of life, but as well we must never lose respect for our elders or caring for one another. The social part of our lives is equally important."

He was on a roll now and there was no stopping him. "Meeting for a chat over a mug of coffee or cup of tea can do wonders for whatever ails you. And with all due respect to Dr. Doolittle and Wallace Bottomley, I believe laughter is one of life's best medicines. Exercise is as important as eating proper nourishing meals. If you can, walk, don't drive! If anyone has anything they'd like to add, now's the time."

There was silence for a moment and then Jimmy O'Connor stuck up his hand. "My hobby is farming, but I don't recall Ben Hong addressing any hobby or skill that he might bring to our community."

Bonsai Ben walked up to the blackboard and wrote, *He who asks, may be a fool for five minutes. He who doesn't is a fool for a lifetime.* "Thanks for asking Jim. I'd be glad to discuss my other interests. They've become such an integral part of my life, I no longer think of them as hobbies." He executed a slight bow. "I'm versed in the martial arts. I have a black belt in judo, and have studied Taekwondo, Muay Thai, Yang style tai chi, and chi gung. I'd be happy to give lessons in any of these practices once I get established."

He pulled a small book out of his back pocket. "This little volume by Chinese author Lao Tsu is called the *Tao Te Ching* and describes something called *wu wei*. I'll leave a copy for Bert's library."

The room was silent and he continued speaking. "If I may say so, it's a principle in Chinese literature that's well worth knowing. *Wu wei* means literally 'to do without doing.' Life should flow with the smoothness of a mountain stream. As you complete a task, it should be conducted without perspiration or exertion, with very little energy expended. Many ailments these days in life are due to stress and practising tai chi does wonders for those of any age anywhere. My sister, Melanie, is qualified in Chinese medicine and acupuncture. She would be willing to offer advice on Chinese remedies which could be sold at Wallace's pharmacy as well as administer treatments in acupuncture or Chinese massage. I hope that answers your question, Jim." He bobbed his head in another small bow and sat down.

Abner Moss walked up to the blackboard and wrote, *There must be something to acupuncture. After all, you never see a sick porcupine.*

That brought a chuckle and Bert stood up and took over the floor again. "I know we don't live in Utopia here, but we have a lot to offer that the world is missing. From the words of the old vaudeville song, 'Let's accentuate the positive, and eliminate the negative.' That could be our motto."

Most of the group nodded at that suggestion and

Bert continued. "I'll end this meeting with two items. In order to retain our hamlet's good points and keep out the bad, we may have to resort to legal methods which would involve instituting new laws. According to Porcupine County bylaws once these three businesses become established, Porcupine Junction will qualify as a village which means we can elect a mayor and council who can pass laws if need be." He didn't stop or ask for comments.

"So during the next month, we'll be conducting municipal elections, and we'll be seeking candidates for mayor and five councillors. Those wishing to run will have one month to conduct their campaigns. The only conditions for eligibility are that candidates are of voting age and reside in Porcupine Junction proper or on one of its adjacent five lines."

A murmur of voices hummed through the crowd. Bert waited a moment and then said, "The last item on today's agenda concerns plans for building. Volunteer work parties will be formed to assist with the construction to house the three new businesses. See me before you leave if you're available. That completes today's business." He gave the milk pail a final whack with the lag bolt and declared, "This meeting is now officially over!"

BeWare oF BearS

From the early days after Bert constructed Nell's General Store and Post Office, the Parkers were aware that black bears often roamed through the woods nearby, but the couple never considered the roaming bruins to be a threat to them.

This impression disappeared the night they were away visiting Nell's niece, Eunice, down south.

On the night during the Parkers' absence, a bear must have gotten wind of Nell's supply of baked goods. When the couple returned to the Junction, they discovered a bear had demolished the exterior door to Nell's kitchen. The animal had feasted on a half dozen of Nell's blueberry pies it had sniffed out, and had made short work of at least three dozen of Nell's famous honey-dipped donuts.

Following the break-in, Bert rebuilt the kitchen door reinforcing it with enough lumber and hardware to make it impregnable to any more future invasions by bears.

The only other such incident worth reporting occurred almost two years later. It was early one morning as Nell laboured behind the bakery counter arranging baked goods on the shelves. She was not quite ready for business, but the front door was unlocked.

As Nell stooped over, organizing the bottom shelves, she thought she heard a sniff behind her. Assuming it was an early customer, she called over her shoulder, "Good morning, can I help you?" There was no reply. When she turned around, she was face-to-face with a male black bear standing with its front paws on the counter and its nostrils quivering with expectation at the odours it inhaled.

Without hesitation, Nell grabbed a broom from the corner, shouting, "Shoo, shoo, scat outta here." She smacked the bear on the head with her broom and bounded around the corner of the display cabinet.

What happened next was best described by her sister Myrtle who was on her way to work to the bake shop that day. She reported what she'd witnessed to Mildred McKay later that day. "I just came around the corner near the store's front porch, when a full-grown black bear came galloping out through the bakery's front door. Nell was in hot pursuit, swinging her broom and yelling. I've never seen Nell move so quick in my life. Nor a bear, for that matter. The two raced down the street until the invader veered off and headed off into the bushes."

Buddy's Dream

It was a blustery second day of winter when Clyde Wopper ambled into Bert's Shop. A chorus of laughter greeted him as soon as he stepped through the doorway. Abner Moss was the first to ask through his Cheshire Cat grin, "What the hell's that on your head Clyde?"

"It's my new hat. Jest what a feller needs on cool day like this!"

Big Jim O'Connor couldn't help but add his own critical assessment of Clyde's new headgear. "It looks like a terrified tom cat just jumped on top of your head, Clyde. What kind of fur is it anyway?"

"It's real coyote fur, Jimmy, an' it's not from one of them endangered species in the world."

Howard Oakley had to offer his two cents worth. "The only thing that's endangered around here is your self-respect fer wearin' a piece of apparel that looks like a giant fur ball that a cat might throw up. I hope you had that thing deloused before you brought it in *ter* here. You'd better not let Nell's hound Buddy ←︎ catch sight of that thing. Although I must admit it would look a whole lot better after it passed through Buddy's digestive system."

As the barbs of critics continued, Myrtle Butler and Mildred McKay wandered in from their morning walk. On overhearing the remarks, Myrtle felt it was time for compliments. "Don't listen to them, Clyde. They're just jealous. I think it makes you look distinctive, like one of them Bolshevik Czars."

Mildred joined in. "She's right, Clyde. You look real distinctive, just like a Russian movie star I once saw."

Jim Butler, who had rocking silently, joined in. "Ya, he looks like a movie star all right. Reminds me of a cartoon I usta' watch as a kid. It was about the exploits of an animal called Wily Coyote."

Assuming the onlookers had run out of caustic criticisms, Bert Parker offered his opinion. "I kinda like your new chapeau, Clyde, but just don't let it get out of your sight with these characters around here. One of 'em might snatch it up when you're not lookin. They would likely try to turn it into Harry Bartlett, the game warden, an' want to collect the bounty that's offered on coyotes in this county."

"Thanks, Bert. You're probably right there. I know these folks are jest jealous of my good looks, especially when I'm wearin' my new fur hat. It's the perfect souvenir from my last summer's trip to Newfoundland. I could have brought home a lobster trap but I'd look pretty silly wearin' that on my head. I 'spect my new fur cap will be mighty useful come winter weather.

Just as Clyde reached the doorway, Nell Parker walked in with Buddy at her side. Buddy's nose twitched. He woofed twice and began to growl.

Clyde reached down, patted Old Buddy gently on the head. "Good dog. That's the most intelligent criticism I've heard about my new hat since I walked through this doorway."

The following day Clyde ran around in a frenzy. His new hat had gone missing. When he went to the post office to collect his mail, Nell gestured a crooked finger at Clyde and pointed to Buddy curled up sleeping on his blanket in the corner. A hint of fur attached to his new hat peeked out from beneath the old mutt's head as he contentedly lay snoozing.

5

AWAITING THE RESULTS

Narrow minds often have wide mouths.
(Myrtle Butler)

When the final day for nominations arrived, there were two registered candidates for mayor: Myrtle Butler, Nell's twin sister, co-owner of *The Dew Drop Inn* back by the fire hall, and realtor, Alfred Piker.

Alfred Piker was a bachelor who lived in a basement apartment in his mother's house out on the Third Line.

Myrtle, who was married to Jim Butler had no

objection to being called Myrt, but Alfred who was a real estate salesman insisted on being addressed as Alfred, not Alf. It was a matter of recognition of his station in the community to use his proper given name.

Alf has been described as being lean and lanky. He usually wore a Harris Tweed sports coat, charcoal coloured vest and polka dot bow tie. He though this made him look distinguished, but behind his back, there were those who thought he looked more like a vaudeville dance man and all he needed to complete his image was a cane and spats.

When Alfred formed his own company and called it *A Piker Real Estate*, his friends suggested that name might give prospective clients the wrong impression about his honesty. Shortly thereafter, Alfred changed the name of his agency to *Four Star Realty*.

Those who knew Myrtle on a personal basis realized that she possessed the same aspirations for Porcupine Junction as her sister Nell. If the truth was known, Alf always was, and always would be a con man. He could be as slippery as a snake in his business dealings, or accommodating when it served him.

Confidentially, Alf Piker's reasons for running for the mayor's job were to line his own pockets. His original company name would have been the more accurate one for his business. Once he was elected as mayor, Alf hoped to press for an increase in the area allotted for residential construction as he was in favour of attracting more industry to the village regardless of any negative impact that it might have on the local environment. Alfred Piker's mayoralty campaign rested solely on the idea of expansion and what he called *progress*. Winning the election would place him in the driver's seat to increase money-making business for his real estate company. Myrtle Butler on the other hand adopted the campaign slogan, 'Leaders Must Put People Before Politics.'

As soon as the starting gun was fired for the election, most voters realized that the two candidates for mayor did not agree in their outlooks on life.

Alf Piker was first and foremost for Alfred Piker, regardless of any other implications.

Myrtle felt that anyone elected to office should have a vision which extended beyond the next election. She believed a leader should have a clear picture of the world and the conditions necessary for the well being of human life. She recognized that the electorate are human beings who deserve clear air to breathe, clean water to drink, and rich uncontaminated soil to produce healthy food.

When Nell asked her sister why she decided to run for the mayor's job, Myrtle replied, "I'd rather try something and fail, than try nothing and succeed." She then went on to say. "Since we're all social animals, we should cherish strong family ties, support the community and value gender equality while avoiding conflict whenever possible. We should act in league with Nature, not outside of it. The village's economy is important, but not at the expense of its environment."

Myrt had obviously done her homework and if the blatant truth about the real motives had been more obvious to voters at the start of the election, the results would have been a foregone conclusion. Since Alfred Piker kept his real motives well hidden, voters had a decision to make. This made the election a contest between an honest realist, and a candidate with a hidden agenda.

During the election, the campaign signs were to be kept to a minimum. Weekly meetings were held in Bert's shop where those vying for office could state their positions and answer questions from any spectators. As one of the first sessions began, Myrt walked up to the blackboard in Bert's shop and wrote, *"The most important thing in communication is to hear what isn't being said."*   There were no attack ads, or negative innuendos allowed during the election.

Myrtle's surprise tactic happened on the first day of the campaign just after sunrise. If you had been up bright-eyed and bushy-tailed, you might have noticed the battered pickup which came to a stop near the front entrance of The Dew Drop Inn.

The lettering on the cab's doors read, *The Hurleyville Taxi,* and on the sides of the tandem trailer hooked on behind were written RUSTY and RED. A tiny red wagon sat perched atop the truck's cab. By noon, the Hurleyville Taxi was fully operational. Howard Hurley, Myrtle's brother, had made the trek from his home in Algoma country's Echo Bay with his two trained Tamworth hogs, Rusty and Red. Howard had been featured in Ripley's Believe It Or Not! and was recognized as the world's paramount trainer of swine.

Professional country musician, Russ Gurr, 'The Singing Farmer' of Brandon Manitoba, had recorded and performed two songs based on the exploits of Howard and his team of hogs which supplied the Taxi's pig power. Following is the chorus of the first song:

Believe it or not, strange as it seems
Two hogs in harness was once Hurley's dream
Two thousand pounds of bacon and bone
But the Hurleyville Taxi will get you back home.
The Taxi was actually a red wagon covered by a

canvas top decorated with a fringe, much like a traditional surrey with a fringe on top.

Howard sported a ten-gallon Stetson, red plaid vest, cowboy boots, and usually wore a broad grin.

His rust coloured hogs' harnesses glittered in the sunlight as the morning rays danced off their copper and brass fittings. During Howard's one week stay in the Junction, he paraded around the streets with a banner fluttering behind, inscribed with the message, "Vote Myrtle For Mayor. She Doesn't Believe In Pork Barrel Politics."

At convenient spots along the route, Howard would pause and give rides to kids and adults or any interested bystanders. He entertained passengers with tall tales, and sang ditties, most of which he composed himself. One of his favourites was 'The Echo Bay County Jail' which began, "I was born in Garden River where streetcars never run. The doctors said I'd never live 'cause I was born too young."

He even passed out coloured souvenir postcards containing a photo of himself standing beside Rusty and Red. At the end of that week of campaigning, Howard and his entourage quietly slid out of town, but not before they had left an indelible mark on prospective voters.

To combat any impact the Hurleyville Taxi might have had on swaying election results, Alfred Piker paid for refreshments at meetings, making sure that all who attended knew that Alfred was the candidate who paid for coffee and sandwiches provided by Nell Parker's general store. Along with each sandwich, Alf had youngsters who worked for him hand out a flyer extolling the merits of his view of progress. The kids also made sure that every house in the area received a flyer, and that one was shoved into every mailbox at the post office. At one point, glad-handing, advertising, and paying for snacks seemed to be paying off for Alf as indicated by an informal survey conducted by his cronies.

At Bert's shop, Myrtle Butler organized what she described as a historical information session during an early promotion event in the election. After all of the spectators that she'd expected got settled, she began. "Since Gary's folks have lived in this area longer than anyone else, I've invited Gary Caboose here today to provide a bit of background of our community."

Gary stood up and stuck his thumbs in the top of his trousers. "Greetings folks. Myrtle asked me to give you a mini taste of the history of our area, so I decided to start with 'The Great Fire' of 1929 and cover as much as I can up to the present. If I leave anything out, you can ask me for details when I've finished."

No one objected, so he started. "My grandfather began to build our Big Canoe Marina a couple of years after the fire had burned itself out. Since our building site was situated near the end of a spit of land, our marina location still had plenty of trees after the blaze. Following the forest fire, the bush throughout the North recovered itself amazingly quickly so that when headman Martin Eagle Claw's band moved down to establish a new reserve location on Moosehide's shore, it was difficult to tell there ever had been a fire. Soon after, Nell Parker and Bert showed up to build their general store, and Porcupine Junction began to evolve."

He pulled a checkered handkerchief from his back pocket, wiped his forehead and continued his story. "About ten years ago, the Provincial hydro ran power and telephone lines to the Town of Raven Lake from the generating station at the falls south of Moosehide. Rather than construct towers overland to feed Raven Lake services north of here, engineers figgered it was better to run a submarine cable across the bottom of Moosehide, then go underground to Raven Lake from here. That was good for us. The cables were buried out of sight so they weren't an eyesore, and we could connect to the lines where they came out of the lake." He sat down. "I think that covers about all that I have to say unless there are any questions."

Myrt responded to his presentation. "Thanks Gary for your brief history."

When the election campaign for mayor and council rolled to a conclusion, it was evident that the voters of Porcupine Junction were more in tune with the sincerity of Myrtle's campaign, and they had seen through the smokescreen of negative possibilities inherent in proposals from Alf Piker. When the final votes were tallied, the electorate selected Myrtle by an indisputable margin of five to one.

The results of the election for council turned out somewhat differently. For the five positions available, four candidates registered, (most possible candidates were probably busy building the new business structures). In the end, Mildred McKay, Abner Moss, and Chef Pierre Bouchard, cook at the Dew Drop Inn, were chosen by acclamation. The four acclaimed councillors talked two of their friends, Percy Boyce and Huntley Carver, into flipping a coin to fill the complement of the remaining council seat. Thus Myrtle was elected as mayor, and all councillors were elected by acclamation.

Buzz off Clarence Calhoon

Jennifer Calhoon was tired of her husband, Clarence, hanging around their tiny bungalow on the outskirts of Porcupine Junction. "You're going to have to get a hobby. I'm fed up of you being underfoot every time I try to get my housework done."

Clarence had heard this many times before. "I know, I know. I'm workin' on something that'll keep me out of your hair."

"Like what?"

"Bee hives."

"Bee hives. You gotta' be nuts! You can't have bees in town. Somebody's sure to get stung, and then we'll be in a mess."

"I know, I know, I've already thought about that so I spoke to Howard Oakley and Big Jim O'Connor. They both said I could put a hive on their property. They said it would be great for polinatin' their crops just as long as I looked after the hives an' they didn't get stung."

"When is all of this goin' to happen?"

"I'm pickin' up a box of bees and supplies from a bee equipment store down south tomorrow. I'll put one hive on Howard's property an' one on Big Jim's. I'll see which place works best for this year then decide where to go from there."

Jennifer Calhoon folded her arms with a harumph.

The following day Clarence showed up as planned at Howard's with two boxes of bees, each of which contained a queen. He also purchased protective clothing, a smoker and enough wood to build a hive for each property. Before long, a bee veil hung down from around his pith helmet and puffs of smoke belched out whenever he squeezed the bellows on his smoker. A pair of vinyl gloves extended up to his elbows and his white suit had protective elastic around each cuff and at the bottom of each pant leg.

Howard stood back a safe distance and watched Clarence at work. "You look like a creature from Mars. Why all the gear?"

Clarence elaborated. "I don't want to get stung with bees climbing up my sleeves, or worse yet, up my pant legs."

He set up a container and upended the contents of one screened box into the top of the hive. A mass of a thousand buzzing bees tumbled out. He dropped in a small wooden box which contained a queen. The small queen cage had holes in each end caked with sugar. Worker bees would eventually eat out the sugar plugs and release the queen into the hive.

"Where did you learn about workin' with bees?" asked Howard.

"Bee Books," Clarence said. "I bought one from the supply store down south and ordered another one through Nancy's Porcupine Quill bookstore in Raven Lake. I don't know all there's to know about bees yet, but enough to get by I hope."

"What are all those black specks on your suit?"

"I read about that. When a worker bee stings, their stingers pull out of their abdomens. That's what those black specks are: stingers, but they don't go all the way through my suit."

"Okay for you, but what about the bees?"

"Well, some of"em do die when they lose their stinger, but not all of 'em and they seem happy enough to die for their queen."

Everything went well for Clarence until he realized he had not securely tied the ends of his bee veil. Several aggressive worker bees were buzzing around around his face inside the veil and in a moment of panic, he yanked off his helmet with its attached veil. In his right hand he held a sharp edged hive tool used for scraping beeswax off frames and prying apart stuck sections. As his flailing arm containing the sharp tool attempted to bat away the buzzing worker bees, Clarence inadvertently gave himself a sizable gash in his left ear lobe. He replaced the top onto the hive then made a hasty trip into the Junction where Doc Doolittle stitched up his gashed ear. Thus ended Clarence's first day's foray into the apiary business.

Until Clarence removed the bandage from his ear, he had to answer embarrassing questions from hecklers whenever he visited Bert's shop, however, his first year in the honey business was in general a success. He gave a few jars of honey to friends and supplied Nell with several jars and combs for sale in her store, thereby earning a bit of cash to help pay for supplies.

There was always the potential problem of dealing with black bears which inhabited the north country, but it was only after his hives had been established for six months that a bear knocked off the top off of a hive one evening and cleaned out half of his frames.

To prevent a recurrence of this, Clarence broached the subject to some of his cronies at Bert's Shop.

"I've given some of you lads the odd free jar of honey and if you expect my generosity to continue, I need some ideers to keep bears away from my hive."

The group tossed out suggestions, many of which were nonsensical until Clyde Wopper came up with, "It's bells, Clarence, that's what you need."

"What do you mean bells?"

"Well you know, like hikers have. What they call *bear bell*s that will jingle as a warning."

"I can't be around my hive all day an' night, jingling bells to keep away bears!"

"I know that. What you need is a trap. You've got a tree near your hive, don't you?"

"Ya, I do."

"Well I know Frank Sattachi has a set of Clydesdale harnesses that are decorated with bells. Frank used to give sleigh rides in the winter but he don't do that no more. I know he'd be glad to part with the bells to anyone who could use them."

"So how would this work now?"

"It's simple. Hang the harness from a rope an' pulley above the hive. Rig the rope with a mechanism so that if a bear jiggles the hive, the harness covered with bells drops down onto the bear, scares the Hell out of him an' 'Bob's yer uncle.' No more bear problems!"

"That just might work. I'll have to clear all this with Howard so he can let me know whenever the trap gets sprung so I can re-set it."

All went well with Clyde's suggestion except Howard neglected to tell his wife Rosie about the bear bell trap. Howard knew that Rosie was out puttering in her herb garden while he was finishing his morning cup of coffee. There was the sudden clatter of bells and an ungodly screech from Rosie. She'd gotten too close to Clarence's hive and her curiosity with bees had triggered the trap when she'd inadvertently jiggled the hive's lid. It took weeks for Howard to get back into Rosie's good books for this little oversight.

Living OFF the Land

The Gear family lived in a log cabin on a secluded side road back in the bush approximately two miles from downtown Porcupine Junction. Basil, his wife Emily, and their six kids: Oscar, Mathew, Hector,

Angus, Heather and Sarah were hardy folks who lived off the land.

The cabin housed a giant stone fireplace for heating on which Emily was able to do her cooking. It contained a cooking grate in the centre, and an oven off to one side where she could bake bread, roasts and other such vitals. There was always an ample supply of firewood nearby so fuel for cooking and heating was never a problem for the Gears.

Basil hunted moose, bear, coyotes, wolves, fox, rabbits and other game such as grouse and pheasants. He also enjoyed fishing, often in the company of Gary Caboose. Basil's kids also often accompanied their father on his hunting ventures and contributed to the game their father bagged.

When Emily wasn't doing her housework, she loved to work in her herb and vegetable patch. This also involved battling and attempting to outwit critters such as skunks raccoons, deer and any other animals with a taste for her gardening delicacies.

One of Basil's other activities was raising Husky dogs which he trained to pull a sleigh during the winter. When there was sufficient snow on the ground, Basil used his dog sled for hunting and also provided recreational dog sled rides for the odd tourist who might stumble inadvertently into the Porcupine Junction area. In a pinch, during the winter, if Clyde Wopper couldn't navigate his school bus down snow-blocked roads, Basil would take the kids to school in Raven Lake by dog sled.

Basil was also an accomplished artist in leather work, fashioning creations from furs and hides obtained while hunting. Some of his unique products included moose hide moccasins, gloves, vests, Jackets and even fur hats. Another of Basil's specialties was snowshoes which included the Trapper styles, round Bear Paws, and the long thin Algonquin version usually reserved for racing. These shoes were handcrafted using gut for webbing and locally cured wood for the frames. He purchased buckles but used his own cured moose hide for the harnesses. Basil provided Garry Caboose with a steady supply of feathers and tufts of fur which Gary incorporated into his famous hand-tied fishing flies.

Every few weeks Emily would announce, "Kids, tonight's bath night," and the youngsters dragged in laundry tubs from the back storage shed while Emily heated water on the fireplace.

Basil enjoyed spending time alone or with friends in his sauna. The sauna building stood just slightly behind the main cabin, and a wood fire heated the rocks onto which bathers tossed water to generate steam. During milder weather, bathers ended their saunas by dousing each other with buckets of cold water, or in the winter, by rolling in the snow. The cries of ecstasy from bare bodies as they received bucketfuls of cold water was usually sufficient to keep at bay bears, wolves or any other critters which might be lurking in the bush.

The one activity in which the kids were most involved was picking blueberries during season. The kids would set out from the cabin, along trails into the bush to their favourite sites, carrying a collection of baskets, tins or whatever container they preferred for their picking. Angus, who was usually the leader would begin by asking, "Well, where will it be today, gang?"

The girls would chime in together, "Let's head for the Seven Sisters!"

Angus would object. "We always go there." Then he would say, "But I guess you're right. That's where the best pickin' is." And off they would troop.

During berry picking, black bears often visited the same areas as the kids. While bears munched their way up one rocky expanse, the kids would be picking on a hill nearby.

The bears might suddenly decide that the kids' hill had a more enticing crop, so they would cross over and the kids in turn would cross over to the hill vacated by the bears. This back and forth switching would continue until the kids were exhausted or the bears satiated.

On one day, Oscar and Gus went berry picking by themselves. After they had filled their containers with berries, they carefully placed the brimmed tins and baskets on the ground next to their jackets and headed off for a bit of R&R to play on some cables near a shack and abandoned mine shaft.

While they were enjoying their respite, a black bear discovered this unexpected cache of goodies and when the lads returned and discovered their loss, Gus was the first to exclaim, "Oh! Oh! It looks like a bear has gobbled up our berries. Now what are we going to do?"

With little hesitation, Oscar was adamant. "We can't go home empty-handed or mom will send us back for refills. Let's hang around here and not go home until it's too late for her to send us back out?"

"What're we going to tell mom?"

"We'll say we got chased by a bear and dropped our berries while we were escaping with our lives."

Although the kids tried to make their near-death experience sound convincing, Emily knew her kids well enough to suspect there was likely more to their story than they were letting on.

One of Basil Gear's other skills was wood carving. Using chisels, a wooden mallet and hand saws, he created a variety of wood sculptures. His preference was for carving animals, but he was also good at carving human faces. He did some carvings by request, but he did many more on his own just to perfect his skills.

His wood of choice was pine but on occasion he used maple, cedar and even poplar. One time he cut down a mature pine near his cabin, leaving at least a ten-foot length of the trunk extending up from ground level. His intention was to carve a native style totem pole containing a variety of animals.

He consulted with Isaac Quail Tail, medicine man of the Moose Antler Reserve, to see what choice of animals would be most suitable. Isaac agreed to cast a spell on Basil's totem to endow it with the proper spirit of the animal world, making it appear more realistic and as if the animals being carved might actually come to life.

Members of the Junction community who were aware of Basil's carving as it was evolving, suggested his creation would be more to their liking if it was actually a nude female figure rather than crows, bears and a howling wolf.

Basil laughed off the suggestion, saying, "Are you lads willing to provide me with a suitable model so I can be sure to get the correct anatomical proportions?" When his question was met with complete silence, he said, "I think I'll stick with my original idea."

It took Basil the better part of a year to complete his project. In the end, the totem included: a howling wolf on top, and beneath that, a snarling bear's head, an eagle head, two crows and a reasonable likeness of the head of Isaac Quail Tail on the bottom. It looked as if all the animals were sitting on his head.

As Basil's woodsman skills improved, he offered courses in learning how to survive in the wilds without the benefit of the usual camping supplies. Such skills as: recognition of edible wild plants, construction of snares and traps for small animals, building fires, development of weapons which ranged from the simple sling-shot, to lethal ways of dealing with larger game such as bear and moose. Fishing gear and techniques was also an integral part of his training.

To make the training more challenging, Basil establishd a satellite campus in a remote region further north. As a base camp, he purchase a log cabin several hundred miles north of Porcupine Junction.

The new campus was accessible by road but it did entail a challenging drive over pot-hole riddled dusty bush roads which ended at the Abitibi River. The only way across the river was by a vehicle ferry boat. Agawa, a local native of the Kewatin Band, operated the ferry. Arriving at the ferry, travellers might find it docked on either side of the river and if it was on the far side, it would have to be summoned. The communication instrument was attached to a tree on the near shore. It consisted of a brass church bell salvaged from an abandoned Roman Catholic Church, and suspended beside it, hanging on a cord, was a blacksmith's hammer.

Several bashes on the bell would summon Agawa across the river with the ferry. The operation of the vessel depended on a cable which spanned the waterway. A winch aboard the ferry was attached to the cable and the device had to be cranked manually. With two bodies operating the winch, crossing the river could be relatively speedy, but with a single operator, the back-breaking winching might take twice as long. The vagaries of wind and current also made the time for crossing uncertain.

Basil always received a thrill, when in the cool crisp northern air, whacking the bell with the hammer resonated from one side to the other across the water. After they'd crossed, the would-be survival students were able to learn their skills in a much more desolate area where wildlife was at a premium. There was always fishing in the Abitibi, but on land, game was more likely to be Grizzlies or caribou.

On occasion, the Department of National Defense would call on Basil to assist with survival skills training with military recruits. A combination of Basil's various outdoor survival skills did manage to generate a novel source of income for him. These money makers included working with Gary Caboose to learn the skills of tying his own unique fishing flies. This facet of Basil's many talents had not as yet reached notoriety for which it was destined.

6

Breaking News

Uncover what you long for and
you will discover who you are.
(Mildred McKay)

Editor-in-Chief, Arichibald Pryor, of the Raven Lake *Suppository News* enjoyed it when his employees referred to him as 'The Chief,' but never by the more familiar term Archie.

The Chief sat hunched in his office chair as he scrutinized a document lying on the top of his desk. With a red pencil he made several notations, dashed off his initials, turned over the sheets and settled back into his chair.

There was a knock at his door, and looking up towards the door's glass window he could see a lady waiting.

"Would you get that, Miz Nodwell?"

The Chief's svelte secretary sauntered over and opened the office door. "Yes, can I help you?"

"My name is Mildred McKay. I'm from Porcupine Junction. I talked with Mr. Archibald on the telephone yesterday about the reporter's job at the *News*, so here I am as we discussed over the phone." Mildred gazed at The Chief, who squinted back at her through his dark-framed horn-rimmed glasses.

With his right hand, he brushed back his long flowing ebony locks and with his left, he pinched closed both nostrils, sniffed twice, and fished out from his shirt pocket a red-checkered handkerchief. He blew his nose vigorously. "Come in and have a seat, Miz McKay."

Mildred surveyed her prospective new boss, mentally summing him up. Her eyes took in the green visor fastened by a black elastic strap which circled his head. The visor cast a shadow over inky black tufts of eyebrows protruding over his glasses, but left exposed a beakish snout and pointed chin. The Chief's lengthy cadaverous face was offset by long flat droopy ears which if they had been only slightly larger would probably have enabled him to fly. All of these idiosyncratic features reminded Mildred of a buzzard.

As the Chief leaned back in his chair, Mildred noted his slight paunch visible beneath an ink-stained apron fastened about his neck. The Chief's greying-white shirt sleeves were rolled up to above his elbows, and a ink stains were visible on the tip of one collar. A complete picture of the Editor-in-Chief could have been a cameo from one of Charles Dickens' novels.

Mildred slipped into the proffered chair in front of the Chief's desk. "What exactly does this reporter's job entail?" she asked.

"Well it's not exactly a reporter. You could call it a feature writer. It would involve preparing a social column gleaned from activities taking place in Porcupine Junction, since that is where we sell a good many of our papers."

"Oh, you mean a gossip column?"

"Well no. I was thinking of something a little more creative, although a little gossip once in a while probably wouldn't hurt. For example, I noticed the election in the Junction has just finished, so you could do a piece on that. You know, interviewing the winners, and losers, assessing the results, and so on."

That sounds like a job I might be interested in. What could I expect in the way of a salary?"

"Well for a start, I'd suggest two cents per word with a possible increase once I assess your work."

"How many submissions would be required per week?"

"Let's start with one. If you could have your typed piece on my desk Friday afternoon, I could use the material in the following week's issue of the paper."

"Would two thousand words be a suitable length?"

"Yes, that would be a maximum, and I may have to do some editing."

"Well, I'd like to give the job a try and we'll see if you and I are satisfied with my work after a couple of months. Do you have a contract for me to sign?"

Archibald fished a sheet of paper out of a desk drawer and passed it across for Mildred to read then sign. After she had signed the agreement, she slid the sheet across the desk and stood. "Thank you for your confidence in me. You can expect to receive my first story on Friday of this coming week."

"I look forward to reading it."

Mildred excused herself and headed outside to meet Jim Butler who had been gracious enough to give her a ride to Raven Lake for the job interview.

Jim opened the car door for her and she remarked, "Considering his lack of social graces, I'd rather call my new boss Archie than 'the Chief."

During the following week, there was a continual clickety-clack-clack, ping, ping, ping of Mildred's ancient Remington as she worked through the typed version of her first story as suggested by the editor-in-chief: an analysis of the recent election results.

Since Mildred had been elected as one of the village's new councillors, she thought this would allow her to write an expose with an inside perspective on the running of the new Porcupine Junction administration.

Mildred didn't feel her new job as *Suppository News* reporter would hamper her joint efforts as a village councillor. She interviewed the new mayor, Myrtle Butler, and the loser, Alfred Piker. She tried not to let Alf Piker's sour-grapes attitude show through in her reporting.

The other councillors, Abner Moss, Pierre Bouchard, Percy Boyce and Huntley Carver expressed their optimism at the future of the village and they looked forward to getting the best for village residents.

Mildred didn't report on Percy Boyce's efforts of battling the Devil drink. That might provide inspiration for another story but for the time being, she'd let sleeping dogs lie. Well, for now anyway. To add a bit of colour to her reporting of the election campaign, she titled the story *Pork Barrel Politics* which allowed her to relate how Howard Hurley and his pair of porkers, Rusty and Red, helped Myrtle promote her campaign ideas.

Although happenings such as Nell Parker chasing a black bear down the main street of the village with a broom was not part of the election coverage, Mildred couldn't help but report on the incident. She also extended the bear story by recounting how a local bruin gorged on honey in Clarence Calhoon's apiary, and described how he'd constructed an alarm system using a set of Frank Sattachi's sleigh bells. She didn't reveal, however, that Howard Oakley's wife Rosie had been a victim of the bear alarm system. There was no reason to embarrass Rosie by such a disclosure.

Mildred managed to put together enough of a variety of stories to allow her to pull together the makings of her first column. The Chief didn't edit out the spicy bits with the result that when the issue of the paper went on sale in the Junction, Mildred received many complements from villagers about her in depth coverage. For future issues of the *Suppository News,* Mildred planned to set up interviews with a few of the village's stalwart citizens along with unusual activities which consumed much of their spare time.

She looked forward to the yearly St. Patrick's Day gathering at Bert's Fix-It Shop. She was sure that this event would supply its share of juicy tidbits.

While Mildred waited for the St. Patrick's Day extravaganza to transpire, Ben Hong's planned Great North Cook-off would provide her with plenty of material for one of her weekly submissions. Her involvement with helping to judge the results and her in–depth interviews during the operation of the contest would give her interesting insight into the whole event.

If Mildred was ever unable to get her stories to Raven Lake on schedule due to inclement weather or any other unforeseen disasters, the Editor-in-Chief had asked her to keep compiling them and filed them away for future publication dates when impediments to publication were resolved.

7

Not Your Average Farmer

Life's tough
But it's a whole lot tougher
when you're stupid.
(Clyde Wopper)

There was little doubt that the residents of Porcupine Junction considered Eldon MacAdoo (known as Weasel) to be less than the sharpest knife in the drawer. Eldon earned his nickname from his tendency to weasel out of any tasks which required even the remotest hint of work.

Although Weasel MacAdoo was deathly allergic to hard work of any description, his usual garb would never give one that impression.

A pair of baggy overalls draped over his gangly frame with a noticeable gap between the tops of his size twelve work boots and the bottom of his trouser legs. This space was usually covered by red wool socks above which red woolen long-johns were clearly visible. Leather work gloves traditionally hung from his hip pocket and you could expect to see a red handkerchief speckled with white polka dots stuffed into the bib pocket on the front of his overalls.

Eldon's bird-beak nose was seldom without a drip, causing him to frequently flourish his nose rag, and his Adam's apple bobbed and weaved on his skinny neck whenever he talked. He had a preference for red and his red handkerchief, long-johns and socks were accompanied by his usual red and black lumberjack shirt. Even his snout displayed a red tinge due to constant attention to its drip. Eldon MacAdoo's hair had a slight auburn tinge to it as well, and his favourite head gear was a ball cap with a red squared off peak, an eagle's head embroidered on the front, and two ear flaps tied up top. Weasel's stained and wrinkled chapeau looked as though it had made at least one trip through the digestive system of one of Frank Sattachi's Clydesdales.

Eldon's hair was sparse, but blondish on the top with an auburn fringe around the edge, protruding at odd angles like the beginning of a robin's nest under construction.

Anyone watching Eldon MacAdoo's ungainly plodding as he surveyed his acreage might easily mistake him for a stork wearing snowshoes.

The Junction folks' attitude was expressed by the likes of Clyde Wopper. "That MacAdoo fella has got to be one of the dumbest birds I ever heered of. He musta got holt of the latest copy of the *Suppository News*. You know—the one with the ad by Four Star Realty?" He pulled the paper out from under his arm, opened it to the Real Estate page and read, "For Sale. Prime Agricultural Land, 48.3 Acres of Rich Soil. Ideal For Entrepreneur Looking To Jump-Start His Career With Hobby Farm (Potential Unlimited)."

Anyone within earshot, would nod knowingly.

"What a lot of baloney!" Clyde added. "Whoever dreamed up that ad musta once bin a speech writer for politicians. Only a bird brain like Weasel MacAdoo would have swallered that BS hook line and stinker."

More nods from the gathering crowds.

"The only crop he'll get outta that hunk of moose pasture is rocks. Weasel can collect enough boulders from it to build a wall all the way from the Junction to Raven Lake. It'll rival the one them Chinese fellas built through their own country."

Eldon MacAdoo knew that folks never figured him as being one of the world's greatest thinkers, but he didn't care. He knew that he was never short of ideas (and some of them were actually good). He was hoping that his latest intended purchase would be one of those great inspiring thoughts.

Between Frank Sattachi's place and before you got to Big Jim O'Connor's acreage, lay a chunk of scrub land that one tended to overlook. It was probably the poorest quality of land you would ever set eyes on fer locating a farm. However, this was, in Eldon's view, the small chunk of paradise on which he hoped to make a future living.

Two years ago, Eldon's parents died and their family, dwelling in the big city down south, was not where Eldon and his sister Gladys-Anne wanted to spend the rest of their lives. The family house left to Eldon included the proviso that Eldon was responsible for Gladys-Anne's future until she married.

After he sold his inheritance, Weasel made the trip to visit his cousin Frank Sattachi in Porcupine Junction. It was while he was visiting Frank that Eldon spotted the ad in the *Suppository News,* and a visit to Four Star Realty was the result.

Alfred Piker stretched a welcoming hand to his prospective client. "Good morning Mr. MacAdoo, I understand that you're interested in one of our listings."

"Ya, I kinda had my eye on that acreage over on the Fifth Line."

"That's an excellent choice, my good man." Alfred breathed a sigh of relief at the thought that he might be able to unload that chunk of desolation.

"Would you like to go and look her over?"

"No, I've already done that. It looks like she will suit my needs All we need to do is agree on a price."

Alf Piker was so anxious to get rid of that headache of a listing, it didn't take long for the two to agree on the amount of cash necessary to seal the deal.

After they had wrapped up the transaction, Eldon dropped in to visit his cousin Frank Sattachi. Frank wasn't as convinced as Eldon was of his new purchase's potential. "It'll take a load o' work lad to get her in shape to grow anythin', but you and Gladys-Anne are welcome to bunk here with Beulah and me until you git yer house bilt."

After the deal was settled with Four Star Realty, Eldon still had a bit of cash left. Frank, knowing that Eldon's first task would be to collect rocks scattered over his purchase advised, "I can help you with the stone pickin' Eldon, May and Martha, my team of Clydes, are always game to haul my stone boat around, but you'll need your own conveyance to do the job as well."

Weasel scratched his beak of a snoz, and rubbed his stubbly sunken chin. "I ain't got enough cash left to buy a tractor Frank. Can you think of anythin' cheaper?"

"This might sound crazy my boy, but Maurice Bass has bin farmin' for years and wants to retire. He has a team of oxen fer sale and I know he'd be glad to toss in a yoke and stone boat with the deal if you want to talk to him."

"That does sound a bit weird, but that'll have to be the answer until I kin get established an' earn a bit of cash."

Weasel knew nothing about oxen, but to seal the deal, Maurice Bass offered, "I'll be available to give you any advice necessary until you become proficient handlin' Isaiah an' Ezekiel. That's what I've called the team since the day I first bought them home. I'd stick with those handles if I was you cuz they recognize yer talkin' to them when you shout out their names."

With the assistance of volunteers from the Junction and natives from the Moose Antler Reserve, Frank and Weasel began picking stones. To supply extra manpower and speed up the process, Big Jim O'Connor showed up with his red Case tractor hauling a wagon.

By the end of a week, they had collected enough rocks to leave several acres workable. Weasel spent most of his time riding his stone boat and driving his team, while volunteers loaded the boulders aboard. He figgered this was the least taxing part of the stone pickin' job.

Gladys-Anne and Beulah brought out a substantial lunch each working day and supplied a hearty meal every working evening. There were roast beef sandwiches for lunch and beef with potatoes and gravy for supper along with a grand selection of desserts.

When Nell Parker learned of Eldon's purchase, she sent out a complementary gift of baked goods to help ease the strain on the struggling farmer's budget.

While the collected rocks accumulated in a pile near Weasel's house site, Frank used his team and a scoop to scrape out earth to form a pit for a basement and foundation. He dug the excavation deeper on one end to accommodate room for parking a vehicle in the basement under the house at some time in the future.

Frank's Uncle Giuseppe, an accomplished stone mason in the old country, had emigrated from Genoa, Italy the previous year. Since Giuseppe offered to supervise the construction of Eldon's stone foundation, he said to Weasel, "I'll draw up a sketch to let you know what I have in mind."

"Great!" said Eldon. "I think you know what Gladys-Anne and I would like in the end."

The next day Giuseppe showed up with a pencil parked atop his right ear and a drawing of the foundation on a brown paper bag. "Well, what do you think?"

Eldon squinted at the drawing as he scratched his nose. "What's that bulge there on that one corner?"

"Gladys-Anne said she'd like a cold room so I made it part of the foundation."

"It looks like the beginning of a silo or one of them round towers they usta build on forts years ago."

"You mean a Martello tower?"

"Is that's what they called them?"

"It won't be as tall as one of them fortification things, but we could put a flat roof on top when we're done. Then you could sit up there in the sunshine on a nice day an' relax."

"With the mosquitoes around here I won't be sittin' out much, but we could put shelves in down below so Gladys-Anne would have a place to store her preserves."

"I'm sure we could arrange that when we're done."

With Giuseppe supervising, a team of volunteers soon constructed a suitable foundation. After the foundation was completed, Big Jim made a trip to the lumber mill in Raven Lake where he picked up enough material to rough in Weasel's dwelling. Since the weather cooperated (with the exception of two days of torrential rain) by the end of the summer, Eldon MacAdoo's residence was sufficiently complete that he and Gladys-Anne could move in.

To complete construction before the cold weather set in, Weasel explained to Giuseppe, "I'm gonna bild two storage sheds to house my team of oxen and enough supplies for the winter, but I plan to contact Mennonites through big Jim and negotiate the construction of a full-sized barn once I have a few sheckles under my belt." Giuseppe's long drooping moustache constantly dripped with sweat while he carried out his trade.

Since Eldon had a bit of spare cash after the house was roughed in, he purchased a flock of laying hens, half a dozen goats, three Jersey cows and a manageable bunch of geese. He also purchased a pair of Highland cattle; the ones with shaggy coats and a gigantic set of horns.

According to Weasel, his theory was that he'd be able to supply eggs for Nell Parker to use for baking and to sell in her store. "And I can probably sell any excess cackle fruit to neighbours in Raven Lake if necessary. An' goat's milk would be an unusual product for Nell's store once Gladys-Anne learns how to milk a goat."

The Jerseys provided him with the opportunity to sell a higher butterfat content of milk and its associated cream, all richer than the product supplied by Cousin Frank Sattachi's Holsteins. He wasn't sure exactly how the Highland cattle would work in. He'd just bought them on a whim because the price was right.

Over time, Weasel's varied pool of livestock allowed him to earn spare funds. He even found he was able to bankroll his questionable vice of chewing tobacco, his preference being Copenhagen snuff.

Eldon MacAdoo had a lot to learn about farming, but one of his proven skills was in expectorating the dregs of chewed tobacco. Eldon was able to direct a glob of masticated snuff into a tea cup at ten paces, taking into account the speed and direction of any prevailing breeze at the time.

One of the goats which Eldon purchased was a crusty old ram which the previous owner had named Jeremiah. But Jeremiah was not just any old goat. Eldon discovered that Jeremiah served as a watch dog as well as monitoring his herd of nannies. He allowed Old Jeremiah complete freedom to roam the property and greet any visitors, expected or otherwise.

As one might surmise, while Eldon MacAdoo was learning the farming business he was not without the odd mishap.

The first was the disappearance of a pair of Eldon's favourite overalls which his goats had consumed while the drawers were hanging out to dry on the clothesline. To make matters worse, the culprits also chowed down on a pair of Gladys-Anne's frilly silk underpants (no doubt for dessert).

The Obstreperous Gander

Eldon's techniques for training some of his livestock were at times questionable. A prime example concerned the conduct of a troublesome gander. The bird had the habit of following visitors while Eldon conducted them on a tour of his farm. The gander would honk, flap his wings and peck at the visitor from behind.

He made the mistake of attacking Frank Sattachi during one visit. Immediately following the first flap and peck, Eldon reached back, grabbed the offending bird by the neck and fired a gob of chewed snuff into the gander's eye. "That'll teach you to stick your beak where it ain't wanted!"

Alas, one could call that feisty gander a slow learner, because apparently he did not learn his lesson as well as expected. Before the MacAdoo dwelling was fully completed, Weasel had friends hand-dig a well for the family's water supply. Eldon discovered that the well also served as an ideal cold storage spot for vitals. He had constructed a platform in the well and a winch mechanism above the well head. Gladys-Anne used her makeshift cooler by cranking the platform to the top of the well. Then leaning over the casing around the well, she placed her goods on the platform and cranked it back down until it reached the coolness just above the water level.

It was during one of these times that Gladys-Anne had cranked the platform to the top and was leaning over the well casing, preparing to lower a chunk of beef into her improvised refrigerator. When she was bent over with her posterior in the air Eldon's troublesome gander spotted bare flesh just south of Gladys-Anne's knickers. The attack on Gladys-Anne's bottom sent her over the rim and onto the platform which rattled to the bottom of the well where, fortunately, it came to a halt at the end of the tethered rope on the winch. The commotion brought Eldon to the scene to crank the platform and Gladys-Anne back to the light of day.

On the following weekend when the MacAdoos invited Frank and Beulah over for Sunday dinner, the main course on the menu that Gladys-Anne served was roasted goose (gander, to be more exact).

It Seemed Like A Good Idea At The Time

One sunny morn, Weasel had hooked his team of oxen to his plow and was cultivating a ten acre chunk of land from which they had cleared the stones. As he was passing bushes along the edge of the field, Eldon spotted a baby raccoon near its den. Since it was time for a break (after all he'd already been out working for half an hour) he paused. "Come here little fellow." He tied the team's halter to a convenient tree branch and picked up the tiny critter, muttering to no one in particular, "This will make an ideal pet for Gladys-Anne. She's bin pestering me about getin' a cat."

He carted the baby back to the house where he handed it to his sister. She placed the tiny animal in a cardboard box and Eldon headed back to his plowing. As soon as he was done for the day (around noon), he returned to the house.

Gladys-Anne immediately asked him, "You are going to build a proper cage for Wee Willie aren't you?'

"Wee Willie?"

"Yes, that's what I am going to call him, Wee Willie."

"Ya, I've a bit of chicken wire and some wood out in the shed. I'll have it all put together for ya by supper time."

From then on, Gladys-Anne made sure her new pet was well fed and she often let Willie run up her arm and across her shoulders while she puttered around doing her house work.

Over time Willie grew in bulk until he was no longer just Wee Willie and the relationship came to a speedy end the morning Eldon awoke to squawking from his hen house.

Investigation revealed that Willie had escaped from his pen and made his way into Eldon's chicken coop. Willie had obviously not forgotten his original wild ways which, once resurfaced, had led to the demise of several of Weasel's prized laying hens.

Later that day, Weasel was discussing the incident with Big Jim O'Connor who offered to solve his friend's problem.

"I'll look after him for you lad. I have to go back to the mill on the other side of Raven Lake today. I'll take Willie along and let him loose in the bush. That way he'll be someone else's problem, not yours."

Thus endeth the posh life of Wee Willie, the wild raccoon.

Joining The Mechanized World

Eldon MacAdoo managed with his team of oxen for approximately three years, but whenever he showed up at Bert's Shop there was seldom a visit when someone didn't ask, "Weasel, when are you ever going to get rid of your biblical beasts of burden and join the modern mechanized world?"

Eldon usually replied, "Whenever I can save enough cash to afford a proper set of wheels."

It was the end of the growing season after

plodding for too long behind his team that Eldon
MacAdoo finally decided that he'd had enough. He'd
saved a nest egg of cash and found a buyer to take
Isaiah and Ezekiel off his hands. Eldon's nest egg was
not quite sufficient to purchase an honest to goodness
tractor, so his choice was the next best alternative that
he could afford.

At Irwin Swent's garage and used car lot in
Raven Lake, Eldon discovered the answer. Irwin dealt
in used cars, trucks and whatever other machinery he
could make a deal on.

One of the contraptions on his lot was a surplus
Second World War tracked armoured troop carrier,
complete with its original Bren gun (no longer
operational due to government regulations).

Since the vehicle had a winch on the front and
trailer hitch on the rear, it didn't take much convincing
on Irwin's part to assure Weasel that such a tracked
machine was the ideal replacement for a real tractor
(and the price was right).

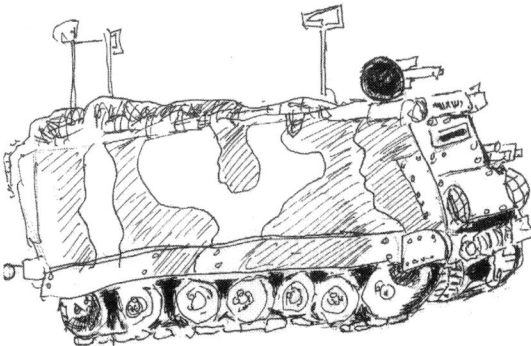

It was certainly a surprise the day Eldon MacAdoo rattled and roared to a halt at the side entrance to Bert's Shop. The slack jaws and gasps of, "My God, would ya look at that!" and "I always knew Weasel MacAdoo was nuts!" were typical responses.

Eldon enjoyed driving his new vehicle, which he christened Nellie. From the driver's seat, visibility was restricted to a narrow slit (for protection from incoming missiles) but if he stood up with his head protruding through the top turret, his visibility was vastly improved, as was his supply of fresh air. Whenever he drove with his head sticking up through the opening, he took to wearing a war surplus British army helmet which a previous owner had left behind.

Eldon discovered over time that his new tracked set of wheels was great for plowing, and other related farm tasks.

As his farm life evolved, Eldon decided that he needed to fertilize his one plowed field to increase its crop growing potential. On a visit to Cousin Frank Sattachi's place, he broached the subject of his lack of fertilizer.

"That's no problem lad," Frank said. "I just mucked out May and Martha's stalls and my spreader's loaded with manure and ready to go. You're welcome to use it. All you have to do is get the loaded spreader to your place and then you'll be all set."

"That's no problem Frank. Nellie is runnin' like

a charm these days. I'll drop by with her tomorrow morning, hook your spreader on and head back along the Fifth to my place. I'll have the job done in no time."

Frank warned. "The only thing you have to keep an eye on, Eldon, is the leaver that controls the spreader's operation. Once in a while the gizmo that controls the spreading engages when you don't want it to. You wouldn't appreciate contents of the spreader flyin' around when you weren't expecting it. But you don't have to worry, I tied the lever down with a hunk of binder twine. You'll just have to remember to untie it when you get ready to start spreadin' at yer place."

All went well the next morning until he was half way home. Howard Oakley's honking from his pickup brought Eldon's journey to a halt.

"What's up Howard?"

"Look back down the road, Eldon!"

Weasel glanced first at the loaded spreader which now contained only about half of its original load of horse manure. "Awe nuts! The binder twine didn't last after all."

With Howard's assistance, he and Weasel retied what turned out to be a broken piece of rope. Eldon made it the rest of the way home without further incident, but this does explain why the grass now grows much greener along that section of the Fifth Line.

An Unexpected And Unwanted Visitor

The summer that the election for mayor and councillors was being held in Porcupine Junction heralded the day that Hector Critter, self-proclaimed preacher from Raven Lake decided to ply his trade. Although Hector had no formal religious training, he travelled from house to house in Porcupine County. Like an apostolic Johnny Appleseed, Hector preached his version of the 'Good Book' to the unconverted in the county. He was convinced that any forest fires which occurred in the North were the work of the Devil and he warned the non-believers, "Repent before it's too late or you'll fry in the fires of Hell!"

Since Eldon MacAdoo had heard about the self-proclaimed pastor's visitations throughout the county, he was not surprised the day the day Hector made an unsolicited visit to his farm.

On the morning in question, Gladys-Anne was away at a neighbour's and Eldon was sitting on a bale of hay in his shed as he contemplated putting off several less important tasks to the following day.

Weasel's musing was suddenly interrupted by the rattle and roar of a beat-up Ford pickup which pulled into his driveway. When he realized it was the Reverend Critter making his rounds, Eldon sat tight and out of sight until the preacher hit the road.

Hector probably assumed the farm's occupants would be in the house so his first line of attack was to mount the step onto the porch and knock on the front door.

The reverend waited for a response, oblivious of his surroundings, however, when his pickup had arrived on the scene, the racket alerted Old Jeremiah as well as Eldon MacAdoo. The canny old ram peeked around the corner of the house and watched the back of the uninvited visitor.

Hector's patience was growing thin waiting for a response to his knocks, but Jeremiah's patience ran out before Hector's.

Jeremiah charged at full throttle and with a resounding whoosh of air from his target's deflated lungs, Hector Critter ascended into the stratosphere. Jeremiah's momentum carried him across the porch and out of sight around the opposite corner of the house.

When Hector looked back from his prone position on the ground, all he could see was the last of his fluttering religious flyers settling to the porch like falling leaves.

Since Jeremiah had disappeared out of sight behind the house, the pastor had no idea what had caused him to be sent flying off the porch. Deciding he had better fish to fry, Hector returned to the porch and bent over to retrieve the scattered literature. By this time Old Jeremiah had completely circled the back of the house and was once again peeking around the corner from which he'd launched his original assault.

The bent over pastor presented a target too tempting for the old goat to ignore and once again Hector found himself launched. This time, with his bible still clutched under his arm, he sailed through the air, warbling, "Enough of this Hell-Fire and brimstone. The meek shall inherit the earth after all!" With those thoughts swirling in his fuzzy brain, the Pastor retreated to his chariot and rumbled and rattled down the Fifth Line in search of other less Devilish sinners to convert.

Once the coast was clear, Eldon picked up a cabbage from a storage bin and wandered back to the house to await Gladys-Anne's return. He dropped the cabbage in front of Jeremiah and patted him on the head. "Well done you old Devil" Then he headed for the kitchen for a drink and snack.

A Better Mousetrap

Eldon MacAdoo heard the scurrying of rats as he headed towards the storage room door.

"Damn critters. I'll get rid of you one of these days. My only question is how?"

Gladys-Anne had been bugging him to get rid of the pests from the day she confronted one perched on the barrel of flour when she went to get ingredients for the week's supply of bread.

"Eldon, you're going to have to get rid of those bloody rats if you expect me to keep going into that shed for supplies. They et holes in the corner of a sack of our spuds an' chewed a hole in the apron that I just finished makin'."

Eldon just shook his head. "I know they're a nuisance, but I need a sure fire way to get rid of them. I'm gonna' go over to see if Big Jim O'Connor can suggest a way of solving our problem."

Big Jim was sitting on a bale of straw in front of his barn when Eldon MacAdoo pulled into the yard in a borrowed beat-up rusted relic of a Ford pickup.

"Well, Weasel, what can I do for you today?" Big Jim was in the habit of addressing his neighbour by this uncomplimentary monicker.

"It's rats Jimmy. I got rats in my back shed an' they're drivin' me an' Gladys-Anne nuts. You got any ideers how we can get rid of 'em?"

Big Jim cleared his throat then hocked a gob of saliva into the dust. "Set down fer a spell Weasel an' I'll tell you how one feller I know solved the problem."

Eldon set himself down on a neighbouring straw bale.

Big Jim continued. "Jerry Monkford had rats what was takin' over his grain storage bin so he caught one of the annoying critters, set it on fire, then let the little pest go."

"Let it go? Why the hell did he do that?"

"Well, when the burning rat got back amongst its kin, it convinced them that the barn was burnin' down, so they all skedaddled. He hasn't had a rat around his place since!"

"That sounds hard to believe Jimmy but I'm willin' to give any hare-brained idea a try."

The following morning, Eldon got set to give Big Jim's scheme a trial run. First, he dug out his one and only live animal trap. After he caught a careless old gray-haired rat, he said aloud, "Now you little bugger, go and do your stuff." He held the rat by the tail and flicked his Bick lighter's flame to life. As the smoking rat's fur started to flame, Eldon muttered aloud, "Does that ever stink!"

However, he was so intrigued with the spectacle, he didn't react quickly enough as the little critter curled up and bit Eldon's finger. Weasel dropped the flaming rat. "You little SOB!"

The sizzling smokin' rat scurried into a nearby pile of straw and before Eldon realized what was happening, the straw roared to life in a ball of flame like a barbeque in the hubs of Hell.

Fortunately Gladys-Anne had been watching her brother's foolproof rat removal plan unfold. As soon as she saw the straw pile ignite, she dialed the Porcupine Junction fire Department which soon arrived on the scene and after a flurry of activity quenched the blaze before it did further damage.

Even though, Weasel MacAdoo lost his supply of straw for the winter. His one consolation was that Big Jim agreed to sell him a dozen bales of straw to replace the incinerated pile. Jim even used his front-end loader to pile the bales directly into Eldon's barn thus relieving Weasel of the related work of piling the bales himself.

Weasel still has rats in his back shed, and is awaiting the discovery of a really sure fire way to get rid of them.

* * *

Eldon MacAdoo had just finished breakfast and was watching Gladys-Anne clear away the dirty dishes. A knock at the door caused Eldon to slop over his cup of coffee. "Who the heck's that, so early in the morning?"

"Probably the best way for you to find out, Eldon, is to answer the door an' see who's there."

With his steaming mug of coffee in his hand, Eldon stumbled to the front door. It swung open screeching on hinges badly in need of oil. Scratching his head, Eldon confronted his visitor, Huntley Carver. "What can I do fer you this early Huntley? It ain't even noon yet."

"I got a problem Eldon. I need to use yer phone. I got myself stuck in the ditch on the Fifth, jest a bit down from the road inta yer place."

"C'mon in, Hunt." The door screeched open as Eldon stepped back.

Huntly entered and continued with his story. " I bin to the market to buy some chickens in Raven Lake. On the way home I remembered there was a blueberry patch near here so I pulled over to park on the side of the road to do some pickin'." He yanked off his hat. "I guess I got over a titch too far so now I'm stuck in the ditch. Can I use yer phone to call Irwin Swent's Garage in Raven Lake? He has a tow truck and he should be able to haul me out."

"No problem Huntley, but by the time you call Irwin an' he gits here, I could have you out of yer predicament. I got a winch on the front of ol' Nellie and once I hook you onto her, we'll have you out in jig time."

"That's great Eldon, but I wouldn't want to put you to all that bother."

"No bother Huntley. I'm always glad to help a friend in need. Besides I may need a favour myself some time." Weasel slurped down the last of his coffee and escorted Huntley out to his drive shed where Nellie, his Second World War armoured tracked troop carrier was parked. "You climb up on the back there Huntley an' I'll get ol' Nellie cranked up." Eldon clambered up on a front tread and disappeared through the open top turret.

With a rumble and roar, Nellie surged to life. Eldon's head poked up through the open hatch. While he was at the controls of Nellie, Eldon had donned the British Army helmet left behind by the vehicle's previous owner. Over the roar and clattering of the behemoth, Weasel shouted back to his (-spacing) passenger. "When we get to the end of my driveway, point me the way I got to go to get to your stuck truck."

Huntley nodded in agreement. Any verbal response at this time would be lost in the racket from the roaring machine.

When they arrived at the pickup, (an elderly beat-up Dodge rust bucket) Eldon reduced his rumbling vehicle to a slightly less noisy cacophonous idle.

He noted the crate of chickens perched near the pickup's open tailgate. Weasel unreeled sufficient cable from his winch to reach the trailer hitch on Huntley's vehicle. "You climb into yer cab an' steer her while I drag you out of the crick. I think that's where your front wheels must be stuck."

Eldon revved up his engine, taking up the slack in the winch cable, and with a slurp and pop the pickup jumped onto the shoulder of the road. The sudden jerk caused the crate of chickens to topple out of the back of the pickup and with a thud, landed on one corner , disintegrating on impact.

From his vantage point in the cab of the old Dodge, Huntley watch a dozen squawking Leghorns flap off in all directions. "Oh Damn! What are we going to do now?"

"I'd say it's chicken roundup time. You stay here an' I'll head back to the house to pick up Gladys-Anne an' some burlap sacks to put the hens in."

In fifteen minutes, Eldon was back with Gladys-Anne aboard the half-track. She had the foresight to bring along a bag of seed corn with which they could hopefully use to entice the escaped birds.

The commotion of extracting Huntley's pickup attracted Old Jeremiah, Weasel's Billy-goat which was left free to wander the MacaDoo acreage. When Jeremiah arrived at the scene of the activity, it was with an escaped rooster perched on his back.

It was a demanding chore, but between Eldon, Gladys-Anne, Huntley and Jeremiah they herded most of the loose chickens back towards one of Eldon's sheds. The corn helped to entice some of the escaped birds into the building. It took all afternoon to round up all but three of them. After they had bagged nine fowl, Huntley said the three loose ones would become Eldon's property.

When Weasel described the event next day to onlookers at Bert's Shop, Abner Moss asked, "Did Huntley pay you for getting him out of the ditch?"

"Ya, I got three chickens for my trouble."

"Well Weasel, you'd better not consider going into the towing business with rates like that, but I guess Irwin Swent will be mighty glad to hear he won't have to worry about any competition from you."

8

Martin Eagle Claw

Those who spend all their time talking
will have no time to think.
(Martin Eagle Claw)

Martin Eagle Claw, Algonquin headman of the Moose Antler Reserve was a big man who was as light on his feet as a cougar. Martin traditionally wore a white ten-gallon Stetson with a skunk's tail dangling from the rear brim and resting just below his shoulder blades. Eight eagle feathers were tucked around behind the Stetson's hatband which was decorated with crimson mystic Algonquin symbols. Martin's pronounced snoz was tinged with a slight rosy glow suggesting to those who didn't really know him that he was a secret drinker. At the corners of his piercing eyes, creases radiated out like cracks chiseled into his walnut features. His shoulder length coal-black braids were secured at their extremities by leather thongs. His usual faded checkered long-sleeve shirt hung loosely over an ample paunch while a buckle with an embossed silver eagle's head clasped together the ends of his Harley Davidson style thick leather belt which in turn held up his faded denim jeans. The headman's most frequently worn footwear was a pair of beaded knee-high moose hide moccasins.

It has been said that with the speed and agility of a ghostly spirit, Martin could follow step-by-step in the footprints of a prowling wolf and tweak the animal's tail just as its jaws clamped down on its prey.

The morning after he'd received the announced verdict of the Porcupine Junction mayoralty election results, Martin Eagle Claw stepped out of the doorway of the reserve's longhouse. The sun was just beginning to filter down through the pines as he drifted along a well-worn path towards the nearby Dew Drop Inn. He circled to the back kitchen door of the boarding house and knocked gently.

Myrtle Butler, holding a full mug of steaming coffee in one hand, popped open the door. "Come on in Martin and set a spell. I'll get another mug of java for myself."

"The coffee sounds great, Myrt, as long as you don't expect me to stay an' help with the dishes."

"'I'm not that hard up for kitchen help. What brings you out so early this morning?"

He handed a skunk's tail and eagle feather to her. "I just brought over a couple of presents to celebrate your election win."

"Thanks, Martin." She held one in each hand. "Would you mind explaining the meaning of these items?"

"Well in addition to being signs of respect, they have both been blessed by our medicine man. They'll help you make decisions in your new venture as mayor. The skunk's tail is to remind you of what I call 'the smell test'.

Myrtle tilted her head and crinkled up her nose. "The smell test?"

Before you respond to any situation, check first on your gut feeling whether there might be a potential foul odour related to whatever you decide. Once you've considered all factors, and have come to a conclusion, the eagle feather is to guarantee a speedy implementation of your decision." He nodded his head and the skunk tail on his hat nodded in agreement with him. "I've used these two items all of my life and they haven't failed me yet."

"Thanks for your concern Martin, but I'm afraid as a politician, with the number of times I'll have to use the smell test, this tail will probably soon lose most of its hair, so you'd better be on the lookout for another skunk in case this appendage wears out from overuse."

"Our people have always gotten along well with the folks of the Junction Myrtle. I see no reason for that to change now that you'e mayor. If we can ever be of any assistance, just send a smoke signal out our way and we will come a runnin'."

"I'll get you a refill for your coffee before you go." But, when Myrt turned back from the stove with the coffee pot in her hand, her guest had disappeared as subtly as the morning mists over Lake Moosehide.

The new mayor refilled her own mug then sat down at the kitchen table to complete establishing priorities for jobs that her new responsibilities generated. Items on her to-do list included collecting taxes, policing, and establishing office and meeting spaces.

The residents of Porcupine Junction had previously paid property taxes to the Porcupine County Administration, but following the election of its own governing body, taxes now became the Junction's own responsibility. Although the new village also received what Myrtle considered to be, a measly Provincial grant as well, making financial ends meet for the village would be a major challenge. Obtaining space in which to work and hold meetings were major considerations for the new administration. The new frugal mayor and her equally penny-pinching council were quite content to seek a location which was sparse but functional.

Having scratched a few options onto her list, Myrt decided to wander over to Bert's Fix-It Shop and toss out a few of her priorities to those present to see if anyone might comment on any ideas she suggested or come up with any topics she might have missed. When she broached the subject of office space, it wasn't long before Howard Oakley spoke up.

"I've got the ideal solution for you, Mayor. As you know, Arnold Watson over in Raven Lake just turned eighty-five and wants to get out of his auctioneering business. Arny owns an auction barn that he wants to get rid of and he told me he'd sell the building for a buck if he can find a buyer who would put it to good use."

A couple of fellas just standin' around nodded to each other and Howard continued.

"It was previously used to auction off livestock, farm machinery, or anything on which Arny could make a profit. The building has great seating that would be suitable for village meetings, and there's space under the bleachers to accommodate offices."

"That sounds like it has great possibilities, but it's too bad it wasn't closer to the village."

Big Jim O'Connor piped up. "Alls you gotta' do

is move it."

Myrtle was quick to respond, "Easier said than done, Jimmy."

Jim went on. "I know a group of Mennonites down south who are great at barn-raising. They could handle the moving job, and their prices are reasonable. They could build a new framework here in the Junction and move the original building over in sections. Now that their crops are in, they'd have the job done before the snow flies."

The following day Myrtle made the building proposal to a scheduled council meeting, and the possible purchase passed with very little discussion.

With Big Jim acting as go-between, he completed arrangements with the Mennonite group, and the new council building soon took root between the fire hall and the sand pit which was the proposed site for a Fair Grounds.

The Mennonite moving crew supplied some additional insulation to make the facility usable even in the coldest weather. Heating the meeting space was not considered a problem since the crowd which usually attended meetings would supply body heat to keep the space cozy and warm, much like cows keeping a barn warm in the winter.

One of the most attractive aspects of the new building was the need for no additional tax increases. To cover the cost of furniture and a few other minor expenses without having to exhaust the village's already meagre purse, Pierre Bouchard, the chef working at the Dew Drop Inn and also a councillor offered to organize a Fish Fry as a fund raiser.

'Frenchy' Bouchard contacted headman Martin Eagle Claw who assigned several of his lads to borrow canoes from Gary Caboose's Marina. The First Nations group hauled in enough perch, pickerel, bass and trout from Moosehide Lake to feed the expected crowds for the planned Fish Fry.

What would any get-together be without entertainment? Logger Rufus McCoy appeared one day in Bert's shop and announced, "I'm lookin' for local musicians to form a band." Before anyone could say anything, he continued. "Mike Merganser on fiddle and five-string banjo aficionado has agreed to make the trek from his taxidermy studio out on the second line. And while Rufus plays bass, two of his conscripted friends are comin' in as accomplished guitarists." He took a quick breath and charged on. "And headman Martin's drummer Cyrus Wolverine is lookin' after the percussion section by convincing two of his cronies to accompany him on the percussion section."

Shawn McGuinty piped up and said, "I'll arrange a step-dance competition."

After all was said and done a good many locals participated and in the end, the star dancer of the competition by a wide margin was headman Martin Eagle Claw.

To celebrate his win,Martin hauled Myrtle Butler and Mildred McKay onto the dance floor and dancing arm-in-arm to the Foggy Mountain Breakdown, the trio put on a spirited performance of step-dancing that would put many youngsters to shame.

At the completion of the festivities, organizers drew for door prizes consisting of three cases of home-brewed suds donated by Ralph Schmidt, and four jugs of vino from Luigi Silvano's latest batch of Chianti.

Just two days after the Fish Fry, a few of the boys were settin' around in Bert's shop chewin' the fat as usual when Lucifer Malarky, a logger who worked back in the bush staggered in with his arm in a sling. Lucifer roomed at the Dew Drop Inn when he wasn't at work.

Clyde Wopper was the first to ask the obvious, "Accident at work, Lucifer?"

"No, I had a little altercation with Mildred McKay over at the boarding house." Lucifer went on to explain what happened. "I guess I should have shown a little more respect." He took off his hat and pulled over a chair. "It all started when I called her Mil-dewed rather than Mildred. Then she asked me to turn down my ghetto blaster and I said, 'Why should I?' After all, I was just playin' some country music.

Mildred told me where she'd shove my blaster if I didn't turn it down, so I guess I made the mistake of challenging her to try."

He shook his head and patted the sling on his arm. "That woman musta taken a self-defence course from Bonsai Ben, 'cause the next thing I knew, I was flyin' over her shoulder and bouncing down the hallway all the way to the bottom of the stairs. And do you know what she said?" He didn't wait for an answer. "She said, 'When you learn how to operate the volume control on that contraption, we'll let you back into your room. Until then, you'll sleep outside with the other skunks'." He jammed his hat back on his head and stood up. "I'll be off work until my arm heals, so I'll have to watch my P's and Q's around the bunk house until then."

Clyde and his buddies enjoyed a good laugh as Lucifer ambled out of Bert's shop.

Myrtle was back in her kitchen working on her priority list while she waited for the boys to get her new office building completed, when the phone rang. "Myrtle Butler here."

"This is Superintendent Reg. Baxter from the Porcupine County Police Detachment in Raven Lake. Now that the Junction's officially a village, I wanted to speak to you about extending our policing duties to cover your community."

"We're a pretty law abiding group here, Reg so we won't be needing you folks wasting your valuable time over here much, but I can talk to you about it tomorrow afternoon, say two o'clock at Nell's Post Office over a mug of her great coffee and a slice of blueberry pie?"

Superintendent Baxter showed up at the post office at a quarter to two the next day with his appetite intact.

Reg was a big beefy man who, because his wife Alice was such a great cook, had not gone without a substantial meal since his wedding day. After wolfing down a slice of pie with coffee, it didn't take too much coaxing by Myrtle to convince him that another helping would go down equally well.

When Myrtle figured she had her guest sufficiently softened up, they got down to discussing the policing issue details. "As you may know Reg, we already have our own form of policing the village. And now one of our new residents, Benedict Hong, an expert in martial arts, has been teaching a few of us self-defence tactics." She nodded to the half pie sitting on the table. "Sure you won't take another piece?"

"Well, just a little one."

Myrtle placed a good sized piece on his plate. "Anyone who might be attempted to misbehave around here never knows who they might be dealing with, so they're pretty cautious before getting into trouble.

Reg dug into the fresh pie as Myrtle went on. "Why just yesterday Mildred McKay took one of her boarders to task to resolve a potential problem. I know what your department charged Porcupine County for policing our area previously, and our council felt that under the improved condition you won't be getting many calls from us."

The Superintendent raised his bushy eyebrows and Myrtle continued. "So we figured a reduction in cost by 30% would be an amount that we could handle."

"We'll talk it over when I get back to the department, but if your fee includes pie and coffee for officers whenever we visit, I'm sure we can come to an agreement." And he tucked the last large forkful of blueberry pie into his mouth.

The Great Northern Cook-off

Once Benedict Hong, or Bonsai Ben as he was often known, had gotten his new Golden Phoenix Cafe fully up and running in Porcupine Junction, he had time to think about the menus he would offer to customers. As he'd originally announced, Ben wanted to provide unique choices of meals which were for the most part prepared from locally obtained items.

He had plenty of options for good substantial meals as he'd gleaned from cooking in the bush camps out west, but he began to think about offering more distinctive meals. While talking this over with Nell and Bert Parker, Ben confessed, "I've plenty of recipes for satisfying meals, but I'd like to I offer something unique. Maybe game and other products which are available locally.

Nell offered her own wise advice to this wish. "What you need to do is to run a contest."

"What do you mean?"

"Just what I said. There are a lot of folks in this area who are fine cooks. They all have unique recipes, based on local products. You could call your contest, *The Great Northern Cook-off* and ask for submissions that are as unique as possible and are based on what's available here in the north."

Bonsai Ben raised his eyebrows and listened to more of what Nell had to say. "You'd have to figure out what to offer as prizes and who would do the judging. And you'd need a set of rules so folks would know what to submit. Oh, and you need to appoint competent judges. Local folks would likely be the best to use."

"I think you've given me a great ideal. What do you think Bert?"

"Sounds great to me," he said. "I'd even offer to judge the entries, especially in the dessert category."

"Well, it's settled then. I'll sit down and work out the details. I can make up signs to post in the windows of all the businesses in town. I can even take out an ad in the *Suppository News* in Raven Lake. Hmm. I might even speak to Mildred McKay about doing a story for the paper about the contest."

After Ben's advertising blitz, and particularly after Mildred's story appeared, there was no shortage of entries scattered mostly throughout Porcupine County. The categories were: drinks, appetizers, main course, and desserts. For each submission, cooks would provide a prepared sample and a copy of the recipe. All submissions would be presented at a gigantic buffet set up in the town hall with selected members of Porcupine Junction as judges. They would fill out ballots on each submission using a scale of 1-100 ranging from poor to superb. The official judges to tally the final results were Benedict Hong, Mildred McKay and Bert and Nell Parker. The recipe's name would be attached to the dish but not the cook's name. In the case of ties, any tie breaking decisions would be at the discretion of the judges. Prizes were to include trips to exotic locations (destinations yet to be determined but hopefully other than Raven Lake); A cook book would be prepared, recognizing all the cooks, and printed by the village secretary. Proceeds from cook book sales would be earmarked for the Junction Treasury t go toward village's property taxes.

After Benedict ironed out the final wrinkles in the details, the following creations flowed in:

Drink submissions:

B&B: a potent blueberry brandy distilled by Luigi Silvano

Zappa: a tea concocted from acorns and tree bark, submitted by survival expert, Basil Gear

Blueberry Zinger: a lethal cocktail created by Ralph Schmidt

Appetizers ran the gamut:

Blueberry-Raspberry Goat Cheese and Highland Cow Cream Cheese submitted by Gladys-Anne MacAdoo

Pickerel Pate and Muskie Caviar: a double submissions by Isaac Quail Tail- medicine man from the Moose Antler Reserve

Fiddling Around: a salad composed of fiddleheads, water cress and local edible mushrooms

Woodsman's Wonder tarts with shells from ground meal worm flour and filling composed of grubs and hopping insects

Main Course delights were:

Honey-Garlic Moose Sausage

Porcupine Meatball: ground porcupine and wild rice

Blueberry Glazed BBq'd Bass

Moose Pasture Supreme Chili: ground moose and baked beans. Caution - not advisable for those bothered by flatulence.

Roast Raccoon: best served with blueberry mushroom gravy

Black Bear Haunch

Squirrel Stew topped off with shelled acorns

Moosehide Chowder: a selection of swimmers, creepers, crawlies and shellfish from Moosehide Lake

Desserts to finish off the above delicacies:

These desserts are enhanced when accompanied with a helping of Gladys-Anne McAdoo's goat or Highland cream cheese.

Blueberry Cobbler

Pumpkin Promenade Custard

Blueberry Cranberry Cinnamon Loaf

Benedict Hong planned to feature the winners on his daily menus on a regular basis. In the end the Great Northern Cook-off proved to be a major success locally and the Porcupine Junction Treasury swelled appreciably from the infusion of cash from the sale of cook books. Bonsai Ben figured that if word of the cook book ever made its way to the outside world, the publication's demand might have to be farmed out to one of the country's major publishing companies.

After Ben had been fine-tuning the contest winners and serving them in his cafe, word must have gotten out to government officials. To this end Benedict receive a special delivery letter from the Foreign Office in Ottawa seeking permission to serve visiting foreign dignitaries with some of the winning meals from the Cook-off contest. Officials felt that such dining would provide foreign visitors with a distinctive Canadian feast. Ben did not object to this request and if the meals were featured in press coverage, it would further promote the Cook-off Cookbook and thus swell the Junction's Treasury even more.

9

The Fall Harvest Time

A really happy person
is one who can enjoy the scenery
on a detour.
(Howard Oakley)

Summer was rolling to a close. Early frost bit the air and leaves were beginning to flutter to the ground. It was a typical Porcupine Junction pleasant fall morning as Myrtle Butler wandered past Nell`s General Store And Post Office. Since becoming mayor, Myrtle knew the three new businesses in town had completed construction of their buildings but she had not yet had time to pay them a visit.

She first mounted the steps of the Golden Phoenix Cafe and tugged open the door. The sign Ben Hong had placed in his front window was typical of his Oriental logic: *Eat Here or We Will Both Starve*

"Good morning Ben. I thought I would drop by to see if you'd settled in yet, and if there was anything that our administration could do for you. I understand that you've been busy teaching one of your self-defense courses as promised."

"Yes and I hear that Mildred McKay has already put some of my lessons to good use." He offered her a cup of coffee.

"Thanks Ben. Just what I need." She sat at one of the tables each with a bright red table cloth.

Ben poured out two cups of coffee and said, "Thanks for dropping by Mayor." He sat opposite and picked up a cup. "We can chat while I plan today's specials. I'm still working at recruiting local suppliers to provide game for my specialty menus."

"How's that going." She stirred sugar and cream into her coffee.

"Pretty Good. Gary Caboose has been supplying me with as much fish as I need from Moosehide Lake, and some of Martin Eagle Claw's lads from the Reserve brought in a supply of moose, venison and other game for some of my exotic recipes, but it will take me a few more months to work the kinks out of my supply chain,. So far everything seems to be going well."

"Glad to hear that." She finished her coffee and got up. "Thanks for the java, Ben. Keep up the good work, and don't forget to give me or one of the councillors a call if there's anything we can do for you."

She headed back out onto the street then on to the Medicine Cabinet pharmacy next door. Wallace Bottomley was just finishing filling a prescription for Mrs. Mary Higgins. "Good morning, Mary," he said as she left.

As Mary was leaving the store, Myrtle browsed up and down the aisles to see what was on display. She reached the front counter. "Hi there, Wallace. I just thought I'd drop by to see how things are going and if the council can be of help."

"So far, all's good, Myrtle. I'm still getting my stock organized, and I'm waiting for word from Martin Eagle Claw's medicine man so I can get the Naturopathic supplies ordered, but so far business is going well."

"Great."

"I'm still planning a First Aid course along with a knitting class and should have them all set before the snow flies."

"I might sign up for one of your knitting classes," said Myrtle. "My husband Jim wants me to knit him a pair of wool socks for this winter. So I suggested to him that he sign up as well and knit a scarf for me for Christmas, but he wasn't too excited about that. Well, I must go now and pop in next door to see how our resident barber is making out."

When Myrtle hiked into the *Clip Joint*, Luigi Silvano had just finished trimming Big Jim O'Connor's sideburns, and was lathering up his face for a shave.

"Good morning,Luigi. I assume that handsome character under that hot towel is none other than Mr. James O'Connor?"

A voice beneath the towel muttered, "What do you want Myrt? Never mind the soft soap. The election's over and it's too late to change my vote now."

With straight razor in hand, Luigi slapped his leather strop with the flair of a professional as he honed the razor's edge to the thickness of a hair. "Good morning, Mayor, I'll be done here in a few minutes if there is anything in particular I can help you with."

"No, that's fine. This is just a social call to let you know if there's anything the village administration can do for you, be sure to give us a call. I imagine that Mr. O'Connor doesn't want me distracting you as your straight razor slides dangerously close to his left ear. I wouldn't want to be the one responsible for him losing a part of his anatomy on account of me causing a distraction."

Just before Myrtle opened the door, she leaned over and whispered into Jim's ear. "Do you realize Luigi signed up for Wallace Bottomley's First Aid course? You know, the one on how to apply a tourniquet and how to staunch the flow of blood?"

Luigi tried to placate one of his best customers. "Don't listen to her Jim. She's just pulling your leg."

Jim lifted the corner of the towel. "Thanks for dropping by Mayor with your unsolicited news, and better yet, thanks for leaving while I've got all of my body parts still attached."

Myrtle laughed and opened the door. "So long Luigi." Out on the street she circled back towards the boarding house and passed Bert's Fix-It Shop just as Howard Oakley headed in through the front entrance. "Good morning, Howard," she called following him in.

He didn't hear her, as he was eying the blackboard just inside Bert's shop. Howard picked up a stick of chalk and wrote on the board, *"You can either complain that rose bushes have thorns, or rejoice that thorn bushes have roses."*

Clyde Wopper, who'd just finished a handful of Nell's raisin and oatmeal cookies raised an eyebrow, "What on earth is that supposed to mean, Howard?"

"Well, it's kinda' what happened to me last year when I entered the Raven Lake Fall Fair."

Myrtle, Clyde and his buddies settled down to hear Howard's story.

Halloween Disaster

"It all really started last year on a typical October morning, with growing crispness in the air, just after the leaves began to fall and my wife Rosie and I were enjoying the Raven Lake Fair. Rosie's nose wrinkled at the smell as we wandered through the cattle barn and on the field near the track where we watched Percherons and Clydesdales straining against one another as they tugged sleds loaded down with boulders. We finished checking out the exotic fowl and were partly through the display of garden vegetables when I stopped and said, "Rosie, would you look at that."

She had no idea what had caught my attention, so she sez, "Look at what?"

"Over there," I sez. "Them pumpkins.'

Rosie groaned. "What's so special about them pumpkins?"

"Nothin'. That's just the point."

"Waddaya mean?" she sez, so I explained.

"Those are supposed to be prize winners, but anybody could grow pumpkins bigger than them." Of course now she could see what I was gettin' at.

"Don't tell me you are gonna' enter the contest next year?" she said.

"Exactly!" As you folks around here know, I don't embark on a project by half measures, and I told Rosie that

"We have plenty of space to grow pumpkins, I need to do research to find a suitable variety, then I had to figger out the ideal conditions for producing gigantic results."

So first I checked out the Raven Lake Library, then I went over to the Porcupine Quill bookstore to see if Nancy the owner could help me out.

A volume entitled *Top Prize Gardening Tips* looked like a good prospect, so I asked Nancy to order a copy for me. She also set me up to use the internet and I zeroed in on Conqubeatus Maximus as the most likely variety for success. I looked up all the diseases that could possibly affect pumpkins, and considered the danger of over-watering and under-watering. Since fertilizer was critical, I also decided that my secret weapon was to be a political fertilizer called *El Torro PooPoo.* Its secret ingredient is cattle manure from bulls injected with steroids, but don't tell anyone that.

After I'd planted the seeds, I worked my fertilizer into my plot, then had Big Jimmy O'Connor and his front end loader pile bales of straw around the site as a windbreak and to obscure *project pumpkin* from prying eyes.

I knew Rosie's nerves were getting on edge one day when she snapped at me. "For God's sake Howard, this pumpkin mania of yours is going to drive me nuts."

I tried to pacify her by saying, "Don't get yourself all worked up, Rosie. I've got the seeds in now, I'll just sit back an' watch 'em grow."

But I had to keep an eye open for invading insects, and I sprinkled my pumpkin patch with a watering can when there was even the slightest hint of a dry spell.

One day, Rosie said to me, "You're spendin' more time nourishin' that crop of yours than I did raisin' our three kids. They're gonna' start callin' you Dr. Spock of the pumpkin world." However, she began to relax when October finally arrived and the fall fair was on the horizon.

The Raven Lake Fall Fair that year was scheduled for the weekend after Halloween and the morning after trick-or-treat night, I wandered out to peruse my pumpkin patch. Rosie said that she then heard the most ungodly screech that would have driven any Halloween spook out of its grave.

Apparently when I burst through the screen door into the kitchen, my face was purple and the veins stood out in my neck. "Where the Hell's my shotgun?"

Rosie was stunned. "Your shotgun?"

"Yah, some bloody yahoos, probably from Raven Lake, got into my garden last night and smashed all of my prize winning pumpkins."

Rosie tried to settle me down by saying, 'Calm down. Let's go have a look at the damage.'

Well, there wasn't a pumpkin left that wasn't smashed. They looked like the remains of a graveyard after spooks had gone on a rampage. The split pumpkins looked like heads with gaping mouths, and holes poked by sticks left leering eyes. I fell to the ground and held my head in my hands. "I guess that's it Rosie. This year is a complete waste of time."

But Rosie wasn't ready to give up. "The Fair's not for a couple of days," she said.

I whined back through the slits in my fingers. 'So what? What good is there about this shambles and what's left of my prize winners?"

She carried on. "Now hold on a minute. Isn't there a Halloween category?"

I said, "Yah, but what does that have to do with this scary mess?'"

Well, if my Rosie didn't just pick up the biggest ugliest pumpkins she could find and bring them back to the house. She spread them out on the kitchen table and soon we were into making a display using several tombstones we'd been cleaning for the local cemetery. With my dear wife's help I created a creepy display using red and green Christmas lights strategically placed to create an eerie Halloween spectacle that we called *Spooksville On A Saturday Night.*

There was no contest when it came time to judge this category and there was no one prouder than

I was, strutting around showing off my first place ribbon.

When the judges called the names of prize winners, I was mystified when Rosie won a first place ribbon as well.

When I asked her what her ribbon was for, she said, "You were so busy moaning about your catastrophe, you didn't realize I was busy baking. I used some of your smashed pumpkins and one of your grandmother's recipes to bake up some prize winning pies."

You all know the saying, "If life deals you a lemon, make lemonade" except in our case, with a bit of imagination, we turned the vandals' prank into our own *pumpkin pie in the sky.*

Myrtle Butler had listened to the whole story, intrigued by Howard's tale and when she thought later about his bizarre experience, she realized this was a prime example of how resourceful the folks in the Junction actually were.

A Crisis Looms

The sun had not yet arisen as Nell worked in her kitchen taking the morning's last blueberry pie from her oven. Her dog, Buddy, scurried into the kitchen through the back door. This was the first indication that something was wrong since Buddy never came into Nell's kitchen while she was at work. He continued to yip and whine as he raced in circles around Nell. Then he headed out the back doorway, then in again until Nell finally followed him onto the back porch. Buddy then ran into Bert's shop where he continued to bark. It changed to whimpering when Nell entered the shop doorway. That's when she found Bert lying motionless on the shop floor.

She knew she had to act quickly. She knelt down to make sure that he was still breathing and then raced to the pharmacy nearby and flung open the door door leading to Oliver Doolittle's apartment on the second floor.

Without waiting to catch her breath at the top of the stairs, she hammered on the door until the mystified doctor, still in his nightshirt, stuck his head around out the partly opened door.

"Come quick, Oliver. It's Bert!"

With that, Nell raced back to the shop with the doctor not far behind. When they arrived at the scene, Oliver checked Bert's breathing and pulse. Determining that Bert was in no immediate danger, he asked Nell. to bring a cushion from the chesterfield. He slipped the support under Bert's head, and while Nell stood watch over her husband, Oliver Doolittle raced back to his apartment to retrieve his medical bag and a bathrobe.

After giving Bert a thorough checkup, the doc and Nell helped Bert onto the chesterfield where they made him as comfortable as possible. When enough able bodies showed up in the shop, they put their heads together.

"Let's pull the hinge pins from that door. We can use the door as a makeshift stretcher." They did that and carted Bert inside and up to his own bed where Dr. Doolittle took over again.

"I'll make a more thorough examination to see what medications he'll need. Wallace's pharmacy downstairs should have it."

A distraught Nell, clasping Bert's hand, nodded.

The doc continued. "I do think it would be wise having Bert admitted into the Raven Lake Hospital where he would receive complete bed rest and more extensive tests."

After they'd entered the Raven Lake Hospital and Bert was conscious, he agreed that a stay there would improve his chances of getting back on his feet more quickly, but he hated all hospitals with their scrubbed sterile corridors and antiseptic smells. The strains on his senses reminded him of death, but he also had to admit that the experiences were also signs that he was still alive.

As he lay on a stretcher after being admitted,

the sharp words of head nurse, Florence Boyle, commanded his attention, "Did you get that pill down your throat like I told you to?"

Bert hated taking any kind of medication. "Pill. Fer Gawd's sake, Florence, it's the size of a ten-pin bowling ball! How on earth do you expect me to swallow that thing?"

"Quit complaining. It's all for your own good. Take a little sip of water and it'll slide right down."

"Hardly likely. Besides, I've heard that taking too many antibiotics might create a superbug in me that could become more resistant to the original drug."

Head nurse Boyle, hands on her hips, glared through squinty eyes at her patient. "When did you get your medical degree that allows you to question the medical diagnosis and treatment of a specialist like Doctor Smart?"

"Dr. Smart. Now there's a misnomer if I ever heard one. What does he know about what I can swallow? He's just getting back at me for calling him a quack when I came to and realized where I was."

"Just listen, you horrible little man. Your lousy attitude is getting tough for me to swallow as well." She swiped the empty glass from his hand. "You do realize that once you're in our care here there are only two ways you're getting out." She paused for dramatic effect. "Feet-first, or you walk out under your own steam." She plunked the glass on the side table. "Your wife told me you might be a difficult patient."

"My wife? What does she know? She's not here to see how my sweet and lovable nature is being tested by the medical staff of this hospital."

"Sweet and lovable nature? You have to be joking. I don't think you have a sweet or lovable bone in your whole body and if you don't soon start to do what you are told, you *will* be going out of here feet first!"

"Feet first? Are you threatening me Nurse Boyle?"

"Threatening you? Keep up your complaining and you'll be wearing a bedpan for a halo."

Bert smiled as he imagined Florence Boyle bouncing a bedpan off his skull. Peering apprehensively at Florence, he decided that he'd better retreat and attempt to regain whatever compassion he could suck up. "Relax Florence. I was only kidding. You can even tell the good doctor that I never thought he was a quack, and that I'm getting really great care from you folks here."

Nurse Boyle held her glare steady and Bert's last glance at his intrepid nurse convinced him that hell hath no fury like an irate head nurse with a hypodermic in one hand and a suppository in the other.

During the following two weeks Bert learned to come to terms with the hospital staff, but when he was released at the end of his stay and into the care of Nell, he found that she proved to be an even tougher task master than Head Nurse Florence Boyle.

During Bert's hospital stay, recovering from what was diagnosed as a heart attack, the crowd of onlookers who usually watched Bert work, took it upon themselves to tackle and complete any jobs that showed up at Bert's shop. They expected no pay for their work and took compensation from the satisfaction they received by repaying Bert for all he'd done for them over the years.

Tests by cardiologists at Raven Lake Hospital discovered that Bert had suffered from the blockage of several arteries to his heart. After a triple bypass and the introduction of a stent, doctors advised the installation of a pacemaker, all of which should allow Bert to eventually return to much of his normal life style. Bert thought it ironic that as much as he hated modern technology, he'd have to allow a pacemaker to be installed in his chest to allow him to regain many of his old ways.

Another Catastrophic Happening

During his period of rest time while Bert was recovering, another disaster occurred to a member of Bert's group of cronies.

Sitting in his usual wing back chair in Bert's shop, Abner 'Specs' Moss was watching Ralph Schmidt replace a set of spark plugs in Frank Sattachi's Massey Harris tractor. Abner felt the urge to answer the call of Nature so he headed outside to visit the nearby outhouse.

On his journey there, Abner passed Jimmy O'Connor heading back to the shop. About five minutes later, Abner returned from his visit to the privy without the aid of his glasses. He groped his way slowly along the shop wall, hunting for his seat in the shop.

Big Jim blurted out, "Abner, where the Hell are your specs?"

Abner's face was ashen. "It's a disaster, Jim. They fell down through the damn open seat hole in the outhouse." Just then he found his chair and plunked himself down in it. "Right now they're likely sitting on a pile of poop at the bottom of the pit." He looked blearily in the direction of Jim's voice. "What am I going to do? They're the only pair I've got. They have specially ground lenses and it'll cost me all of my savings to get them replaced, not to mention how long it would take."

Ralph and Jim looked at each other and shook their heads.

Specs wrung his hands and spoke again. "Can you fellas think of any way we can fish them out of there?"

Jim 's eyes flashed. "I think fish is the operative word, Abner. I once read a story about a lawyer on a fly fishing trip. After a night of drinking, he threw up in an outhouse and lost his dentures into the same type of mess into which you lost your glasses. They eventually retrieved his choppers using a fishing pole with attached hook line and sinker. Maybe we can do the same for your spectacles."

Specs Abner looked hopeful. "Do ya think that'd work?"

Jim got up. "I'll get Nell to phone Gary Caboose. He's the best one around here when it comes to fishing. First, I'll get a flashlight from Bert's store, and go and have a look to see if I can spot your glasses."

Jimmy returned a few minutes later. "They're down there alright, Abner, I'd guess, about eight feet, right at the bottom. I could see the glitter of the frames when I shone the light down. Nell phoned Gary. He thought it was some kind of prank we were pulling on him, but Nell finally convinced him that we were serious."

About ten minutes later Gary Caboose showed up with a short fishing pole in one hand and a bag of sinkers hooks and line in the other. Big Jimmy O'Connor took control of the project. "There's only room enough in the privy for Gary and me. He can look after the fishing and I'll tend to the light. Gary fished for the glasses for approximately one-half hour then he and Jim exchanged jobs for another thirty minutes but without success. Ralph Schmidt and Howard Oakley each took a turn to spell off Gary and Jim. Finally after the groups had been trolling in the outhouse's nether regions for about two hours, Gary got lucky and managed to snag the nosepiece of Abner's specs. He carefully hoisted the glasses high enough that Jim could reach down and latch onto them. It was after supper and beginning to get dark by the time they had retrieved Abner's glasses and he was able to breathe a sigh of relief and clean them off so he could see clearly once again.

The following day when Abner returned to the shop, he received a small decorative gift box containing two clothes pins and a note. The note read: "Instructions for spectacle safety: Clip glasses to ears when answering, the call of Nature!"

The humour of being told of the gang's response to Abner's predicament did wonders to bolster Bert's spirits. It was not long after the incident that Doc Doolittle gave Bert permission to resume limited duty in his shop.

When Roving Reporter Mildred McKay heard about Abner Moss dropping his specs through the seat of Bert Parker's outhouse, she couldn't resist reporting on the incident in the Raven Lake *Suppository News*.

Would this be considered to be the type of event that Archibald Pryor had in mind that for her social column? Mildred felt that it was certainly an incident that would catch the eyes of other Porcupiners.

As she'd predicted, it dramatically increased the sales of the *News* in the Porcupine Junction area when the item appeared .

Reports of Bert Parker's heart attack and his recovery were a much more serious story, but one that was in stark contrast to the outhouse incident. Mildred wasn't aware of Bert's encounter with Head Nurse Florence Boyle, but I'm sure that if she had been it, would probably have become a feature story as well.

One could debate whether writing about Abner's mishap in the outhouse was a report in good taste or not, but the response of villagers who read the story convinced Mildred she was on the right track with stories that readers were interested in and thus increase the paper's sales in the Junction.

10

BLOW, BLOW THOU WINTER WINDS

Doubt is the beginning,
not the end, of wisdom.
(Gary Caboose)

By mid-November there was a chill in the air and little doubt that winter was well on its way. In anticipation of a long cold season, Bert had the lads install a wood stove in his shop to take the chill off his work space. Even though Doc Doolittle had advised his patient to take it easy, Bert Parker was a hard person to convince to slow down. Prior to his attack, Bert had been restoring a hard-topped 1929 Model A Ford Roadster.

The first day that Bert showed up for work, Clyde Wopper found him staring off into space. "What are you thinking about, Bert?" he asked.

"While I was resting in recovery, I had a lot of time to think and I got the inspiration to modify my Model A. By replacing its front wheels with skis and using the rear wheels to supply power to a pair of drive belts, I'm thinkin' that would do the trick to propel my dream machine through the snow."

The more Bert thought about the idea, the more ideas arose. He phoned Jim O'Connor for a special request. "Jimmy, will you scoot out to the Raven Lake junk yard and retrieve the drive belts from an abandoned farmer's combine. for me?

"Sure thing."

Bert continued. "I know the belts are still out there and if I wrap them snugly around the drive wheels on the rear axle of the machine I'm buildin' those missing parts will be exactly what I need to supply its power."

Now Jimmy had heard of Bert's fantastical idea and asked him what he was going to call it.

"I'm not sure what to call my snow buggy just yet, Jimmy, but I 'spect I'll get some novel suggestions from the onlookers in my shop."

And sure enough, as he worked on his project, he received all kinds of weird and wonderful advice from the crowd in his gallery. Whenever possible, he tried to incorporate their suggestions, no matter how bizarre, into the scooter's design.

During the modifications to his Model A, Bert

was having difficulty with the tension on the drive belts to the rear wheel assembly. When he sought suggestions to deal with the problem, Clarence Calhoon, perched on a foot stool offered what he thought was sound advice.

"I think I know what will solve your problem, Bert. We yousta own an old Beatty Wringer washing machine. If you ran your drive belts through a set of rollers like we had on that washer, I think that would keep your belts at the right tension."

"Even if that would work, Clarence, where on earth could I get a set of Beatty washing machine rollers in this day and age?"

Clarence had a ready answer. "Abe Silverman who runs the Antique Store over in Raven Lake had a couple of those old machines on display. Come to think of it, I think that one of them is a Beatty, and I know that he has spare parts hanging around as well. I'll go over tomorrow and have a look-see if he has anything that you could use."

Two days later, Clarence showed up in Bert's Shop with his hands full. "Try these, Bert and see if this solves your problem." He held a set of old Beatty rollers and enough parts for Bert to complete the installation.

With a good deal of ingenuity and persistence, Bert managed to run his drive belts between the rollers, and there were plenty of extra parts allowing him to adjust the belts' tension. "What did Abe charge you for these parts, Clarence?"

"Nothin'. He gave the stuff to me in exchange for some old crocks that my grandmother left us when she died two years ago."

By early December, Bert had completed his machine to the point that he could give it a trial run in a light layer of newly fallen snow. With the usual crowd of onlookers at the shop, Bert turned the key, pressed the starter, and the vehicle putt-putted to life. He pulled his contraption out through the double doors of his shop to the slap, slap of the combine belts on the frozen ground. The odd-looking drive wheels on the rear of the Model A gave it the look of an ungainly giant insect as it nudged its way through the snow.

This prompted Clarence Calhoon to shout, "Why don't you call her the Snow Spider, Bert?"

After shifting through the gears several times Bert announced, "Well she at least runs forward and backward on command so I'll pull her back into the shop so I can make a few minor adjustments. Then I'll take her on a more prolonged scoot around the outside of the shop. I can hook on the trailer I built as well. There's space in there for my tool box, containers of nuts and bolts, a couple of blankets, two coils of rope, a roll of stout wire and two pairs of snowshoes.

Approximately two weeks later, a group which included Bert, Ralph Schmidt and Jim Butler were standin' around admiring Bert's creation.

Bert said, "Well, pile in boys and let's give her a longer run with the trailer attached."

Snow along the side roads had accumulated to a depth just above the level of the Spider's radiator cap. With Bert at the wheel, the vehicle crashed through snowdrifts leaving a swathe in its wake as it plowed through the winter wilderness. They travelled along the First Line past Rufus McCoy's taxidermy studio, then across country to the Third line and then to the Tenth before returning back to the shop.

Since the machine had performed so well during the test run, Bert decided to quit fiddling with adjustments and store the old girl in the covered structure, which some of the lads had constructed and attached to one side of his shop.

By the end of January, it had been snowing steadily for well over a month, and many of the roads had became impassable due to the blizzard conditions and deep drifts.

Doc Doolittle was one doctor who still made house calls, but the horrible road conditions made fulfilling any out-in-the country request out of the question.

Bert had been bragging about successfully road-testing his Snow Spider, when Doc Doolittle received three emergency wilderness calls in the same general area. The Doc's only solution to get to those life threatening cases was to appeal to Bert Parker so he wandered over to Bert's Shop.

"I gotta ask you Bert, will you bring your snow machine out and help me treat some critically ill folks? You've got the only possible means of transportation for me to get out to see them."

When Oliver Doolittle appealed to Bert for necessary transportation to complete his three emergency calls out on the Second and Fifth Lines, it didn't take much convincing for him to accept the doctor's request. Bert felt like a kid with a new toy whenever he puttered around in his Spider, but once he'd made the decision to transport Doc Doolittle, he thought it would be a good idea to have another person along so he asked Ralph Schmidt to accompany him and the doc.

After completing the three emergency calls, the scooter was racing down the Fifth Line towards the home stretch when the engine coughed, sputtered, and died.

Bert leaned towards Ralph. "We've been out for most of the day so we better resolve this problem pretty quick. It won't be long before darkness sets in."

It was with this sense of urgency that as soon as his contraption drifted to a stop, Bert jumped out of the shelter of the cab and opened the left side of the vehicle's hood. He tinkered with a few electrical wires and checked the right side before climbing back inside.

He turned the key and the starter coughed and spluttered. Bert's attempts to revive his machine resulted in a few half-hearted growls. "You ornery cuss.! Don't just set there sputtering. Keep runnin' like you're supposed to."

But no amount of complaining did any good to resolve the problem. Bert sat for a few minutes scratching the bridge of his nose as in his mind ran through the list of possible reasons for the problem. He muttered aloud, "I gotta be missing something but I can't place my finger on it."

Perspiration ran down his back even though the temperature was well below freezing and the more he thought about the grave situation and the safety of his passengers, the more he sweated.

11

A Season of Challenges

If you find yourself in a hole,
the first thing to do
is stop digging.
(Big Jim O'Connor)

After Bert's scooter died in the snow, he puzzled over his dilemma for what felt like an hour but it was probably no more than ten minutes, and still he hadn't been able to solve it. The blizzard was making no attempt to abate but somewhere in the back of his mind a solution niggled at him. He continued to grapple with his predicament, which made him more determined to perform another thorough assessment of his machine's problem. There had to be a logical reason for the Spider dying

Ralph had taken a turn on it as well, and with a

wail of exasperation exploded. "Come on Bert. Let's give it one more try. Surely, between the two of us we can figure out what the problem is before the Spider — and we—get completely buried in the teeth of this gale."

After more tinkering and prodding, and much musing, Bert had a hunch to use the handle of the hammer to tap the gas tank. Each tap emitted a dull thunk. "Just what I figured," he said. "We're out of gas."

They climbed back into the cab out of the blowing snow and Bert said, "I haven't had enough chance to drive the old girl to see how much fuel she actually used and I guess bucking those snow drifts took a lot more petrol than I expected." He banged a gloved fist into his other hand. "And I thought of most everything to bring, except the obvious—a jerry can of gasoline."

"We'll we do have snowshoes and I can make it back to your shop. I know a shortcut through the bush over there."

Bert knew he shouldn't attempt it and said, "But the snow hasn't let up. Are you sure you can make it?"

"I can do it. The back road is just beyond those trees. I'll hike back to the shop, and pick up a can of gas and be back within the hour."

Bert watched the bent figure push into the wind as Ralph trudged back to the trailer. He pulled out a pair of snowshoes, strapped them on and disappeared into a wall of swirling white snow.

It took two hours for Ralph to get back with the can of fuel and when Bert saw his puffing and plodding friend stumble out of the drifting snow, he breathed a sigh of relief.

He jumped out and took the can from his snow encrusted friend. "I'd begun to wonder if you'd gotten lost," he yelled. "Glad to see you back." And as Ralph climbed into the shelter of the cab, Bert quickly filled the scooter's tank.

With the fuel added, Bert coaxed his tiny four cylinder engine to cough to life then purr along without missing a beat. They covered the distance back to the shop in a little more than half an hour. As he pulled the scooter into its storage shed, he vowed he'd just made his last trip for that winter.

As soon as Bert slammed the door on the Spider, Doc Doolittle shuffled off homeward. "I'm looking forward to a hot dinner which I'm sure my wife still has waiting for me." He shivered and hugged his arms close. "Of course that's after I quench my thirst with a hot brandy to celebrate the end of this ordeal and get my blood circulating again."

Now that the emergency trip was over, Bert spent more time thinking about how residents of the area made the best use of the winter season. Over the years the locals had become well adapted to deal with the bitter cold weather. Residents of the Junction enjoyed cross country skiing and snowshoeing while the kids played shinny on the ice covered ponds. Dressed for bitter freezing temperatures, kids kept warm by playing hockey. They weren't the least bit concerned about the year's growing drifts. The little nippers just kept clearing their ice surfaces and playing more and longer hockey games. Those kids who couldn't afford proper hockey equipment taped magazines to their legs as shin guards and used horse droppings as pucks.

When Bert Parker had completed the construction of his unique Snow Spider, Roving reporter Mildred McKay took that as an opportunity to create another story about the machine's construction. She also included an account of his medical mission when Bert transported Doc Doolittle on his medivac life-saving mission into the hinterlands of snowbound Porcupine County.

As Mildred continued to write weekly stories for the Suppository News, stories such as Bert Parker's creation of the Snow Spider and its use to benefit others in the community, she came to recognize how unique the village of Porcupine Junction actually was.

Once, when Bert was day-dreaming, he began to think back to the time several weeks before

Christmas when he'd walked in on Nell in a heated conversation with her sister Myrtle. They were standing at the counter in Nell's General Store discussing the Christmas Concert that was being proposed for the new village hall. The main topic under discussion was who would portray Santa Claus for that coming performance.

Myrtle was forcefully expressing her opinion. "In spite of one slight flaw in his character, Percy Boyce should go down in our history as the greatest Santa ever in this area."

Nell Parker slammed a ham-sized fist onto the counter. "Not in my dang books he ain't. That one small flaw in his character you're talkin' about will catch up with him someday soon, just as sure as my name's not Missus Claus." She chose to overlook the fact that any opinion she had about Percy was due to her being one of the Junction's staunchest most vocal teetotalers. "Don't you recall what happened? When it was time to say his lines at the end of last year's concert in Raven Lake? He staggered onto the stage and slurred, 'I wush youses a furry murry Christmess', or words to that effect. Then he fell off the stage into my lap since I was sittin' in the front row."

Myrtle responded."Well I suppose you're partly right Nell, but I don't think that what happened was all Percy's fault. According to what I heard, he stepped outside for a break while he was waitin' to say his piece at the end of the show and he met up with Joe Snell, our Fire Chief, who just happened to drop by to pick up his daughter when the concert was over."

Nell just grunted so Myrtle continued the story. "Joe had a jug of Demerara rum that he'd just purchased to spike his wife's Christmas eggnog. By the time Percy an' Joe finished sippin' the Demerara, there was hardly enough left to spike even a thimble full of any Christmas drink. I say it was Joe's fault more than Percy's for what happened."

Nell smirked. "I guess you have a point there Myrtle, but I still think one's as bad as t'other."

Myrtle then got on about how great Percy was at being Santa. "He's built just right for the part. Doesn't need stuffin' for his suit. Remember they tried that skinny Ralph Baxter one year? He looked more like an underfed scarecrow than a Jolly Santa. Besides, Percy has that perfect crop of snowy white hair and his bushy beard and moustache are just right for the part." She slapped her knee. "Even his red nose reminds kids of Rudolph."

Nell couldn't help to get back to picking holes in Myrtle's argument, reminding her, "Don't forget the main reason for Percy's red nose is due to his drinking problem."

"But if not Percy, who will we get to be Santa Claus this year?"

Nell came up with what she thought was the ideal solution, "I'll just have to twist Clyde Wopper's arm to get him to do it. He's certainly built for the part."

"Well, you're right about that," Myrtle said. "It won't take a load of stuffin' to get his suit padded. But we'll need to buy him a bushy set of whiskers and whiten up that red 'tache of his." She gathered up her shopping bag full of groceries. "I havta say, I'll look forward to seeing Clyde in action at our concert this year Nell." And with a grin, she stomped out the door.

The committee then made all the arrangements for their first Christmas Concert based on the assumption that Clyde Wopper would be their Santa.

On the day for which the concert was scheduled, it was cool and snowing lightly, ideal weather for the Christmas season. Clyde bustled around getting ready to leave his house to walk over to the new village hall for the concert while his wife kept nagging him. "Are you sure you know your lines, dear?"

"Ya, I'm all set Joyce, quit buggin' me. I know what I have to do and I've got lotsa time before the concert starts."

Since Clyde wasn't keen in the first place to play Santa and was in no rush to get to the concert early, he thought he'd drop in at Joe Snell's place for a social visit. Besides, Joe's house was on the way to the hall.

Wearing his bathrobe and slippers, Joe Snell answered the door and ushered Clyde inside with an invitation to sample his wife's eggnog. "I'm not sure if Bertha added enough rum, Clyde, but give it a try and tell me what you think."

After downing several samples and suggesting an increase in potency after each, a well-lubricated Clyde finally set out for the concert. Both his beard and toque were slightly askew and his posterior stuck out farther than usual. Even his snout had taken on a bit of a rosy glow. By this time, his gait resembled that of a sailor weaving across the deck of a rolling ship.

When the time came to give his lines, Clyde was feeling no pain so his speech was punctuated by several hiccups, belches and a few choice four-letter expletives. He forgot to wish the audience a Merry Christmas and his last words as he lurched off the stage were, "Cheers, cheers, bring on the beers! Now that thush perrrfooormunce is over, I'm outta' here. Merry Reindeer To All!"

Roving Reporter, Mildred McKay, was present for the Christmas Concert where she viewed Clyde Wopper's inebriated performance as Santa Claus. How could such a dedicated reporter avoid creating a story from such a novel performance? After all, wouldn't one consider it as an integral part of Porcupine

Junction's social calendar? It was certainly an incident worth reporting on. If that wouldn't sell papers, what would?

And so she wrote about the story behind the Clyde Wopper incident. The community as a whole didn't realize that Clyde had stumbled into his soused Santa performance as a result of extenuating circumstances, that being the presence of Joe Snell and his wife's spiked egg nog.

Following Clyde's inebriated performance, the concert organizers decided unanimously that they could live with Percy Boyce's shortcomings, and voted to recruit him to be their future Santa on a permanent basis. Perhaps this was partly due to Mildred's story in the *Suppository News*?

12

Gettin' The Year OFF To A Good Start

Even though a number of people have tried, no one has yet found a way of drinking for a living.
(Ralph Schmidt)

The advent of spring marked two seasonal events in the vicinity of Porcupine Junction. The first was the collection of sap to be boiled down into maple syrup. This resulted in one more chore for Howard Oakley who managed a small scale maple syrup business which provided him with cash for luxuries which he could otherwise not afford. He managed to collect a sufficient amount of sap to provide Nell Parker with several jugs to sell at her store.

Howard placed spigots in the trunks of maple trees in the bush adjacent to his house and collected the sap in buckets, and boiled it down over an open wood-fired blaze in his yard. He could have used plastic lines and a pump to increase the scale of his operation, but he was quite content to keep his syrup business a modest one.

To supplement that which she bought from Howard, Nell also purchased maple syrup from the Algonquin Band of the Moose Antler Reserve.

A second event which occurred when March arrived was when the Irish members of the community were up for a St. Patrick's Day celebration. This year festivities, taking place on the evening of March 17th, were scheduled to last for five hours from dinner hour to about midnight in Bert's Shop. One of the earliest celebrants to arrive for the gathering in the shop was taxidermist Mike Merganzer. He pulled up in his pickup which he parked beside the shop, and struggled in with an item covered by a blanket.

Clyde Wopper and Ralph Schmidt were the only two who managed to arrive before Mike. Clyde was helping Ralph lug in several cases of his version of Guinness Stout which was tinted a bilious green to match the occasion. When Clyde and Ralph met Mike at the door with his hidden object, Clyde couldn't help but ask, "What did you bring this year Mike, a stuffed leprechaun?"

"No, it's something more interesting than that."

The blanket covering the mystery item fell to the floor revealing a moose head with the largest set of antlers that Clyde had ever seen. "It's for tonight's festivities for a game I call, 'The Loose Moose-Toss.' The first thing we need to do is put a hook on the inside wall just above the front entranceway. That's where I'll hang my trophy head."

To make the moose-toss challenge more interesting, Mike had fitted his creation with a set of artificial crossed eyeballs, which looked crazily towards one another.

Mike proceeded to explain the rules of the competition. "At the beginning of the evening, we'll collect an undecided amount of cash from those who wish to participate. I have assigned a numerical value to each antler point.

"But what the heck will we use to toss at that dang thing?" Clyde asked.

"I've got that figgered out. Bert is supplying a green derby which participants will toss at the rack and Abner Moss has agreed to tally up scores during the evening.

"How's he gonna see who scored what?" Ralph asked. "It's kinda high up there."

"I thought a that too," Mike answered. "Bert will provide a step ladder to make score tallying more accurate. At midnight,the competitor who has accumulated the most points will be awarded the collected prize money."

During the evening a few jugs of Jameson's and Bushmill's more potent Irish spirits surreptitiously appeared as well for consumption by the assembled crowd.

Along with the Loose Moose-Toss, as in any such gathering in The Junction, music played a significant part. As might have been expected, Mike Merganzer broke out his fiddle and 5-string banjo and his Irish tunes inspired Shawn McGuinty to polish the dust off his dancing brogues and shuffle to a few jigs and reels while he was still sober. There were no shortage of shamrocks in evidence that evening, along with buttons proclaiming "Kiss Me. I'm Irish.'

Even Martin Eagle Claw put in a brief appearance when he heard there was a shindig going on. To mark the occasion, several fluorescent green feathers graced his Stetson. When Mike asked him about his added colour, he replied, "My brother Sasquatch Sam sent me up a batch of parrot feathers from his home near Lake Okeechobee down in Florida."

To be sure that the Loose Moose-Toss point count was accurate, Abner Moss periodically climbed the ladder which Bert provided to check the tallying. This was important to Abner because he thought he'd figger'd out the secret of the game. "If keep my toss totally relaxed," he said, "I'll have a greater degree of success at the game. But I got a little worried when I saw Jim Butler, overindulging in liquid Irish cheer, was also becoming totally relaxed and beginning to catch up to my score."

When the game was over, however, due to his consumption of refreshments, Jim Butler had become more tipsy and consequently better. But at midnight, after Jim passed out, Abner was in fact the winner.

One of his buddies exclaimed, "Your success Abner was only due to the fact that you're as cross-eyed as the moose head hanging there on the wall."

When St. Patrick's Day came to a close, Mike donated the trophy head to Bert to add to the decor of his shop. From that St. Patrick's Day onward, whenever Bert worked on a job, he found it unsettling to look behind him and have the ever present cross-eyed moose looking over his shoulder.

During Bert's St. Patrick's Day celebration, reporter Mildred McKay made sure she was in attendance. She avoided indulgence in any alcoholic refreshments so that she could keep a clear head to prepare an accurate account of what went on. Her article included coverage of the Loose Moose-Toss and who was the winner. She was not a sports reporter for the *Suppository News*, but she rationalized that the Toss fit into the social status of the Junction.

In all of the stories that she wrote for the *Suppository News,* Mildred sought to inject a hint of humour whenever she could. She realized that Editor-in-Chief, Archibald Pryor's, sense of humour was probably on a par with that of a mortician, but one of Mildred's aims in her reporting career was to slowly chip away at The Chief's glacial funny-bone. She went about this process in such an insidious and deft fashion, Archie didn't even realize what was happening to his psyche. Mildred knew that she was gaining some degree of success in her efforts when she once actually saw The Chief smile at something she'd written.

13

It's Going To Be A Scorcher

Success seems to be largely a matter
of hanging on after others have let go.
(Mildred McKay)

According to meteorological records, spring in the North Country was one of the driest in the past half century. Department of Forestry officials banned camp fires and cautioned travellers to avoid the use of open flames. After two months of continual drought, a thunderstorm several hundred miles north of Porcupine Junction seemed to offer promise of a break in the dry cycle, but a lightning strike from the storm caused a tinder dry dead Blue Spruce to burst into flame. This seemingly minor incident initiated a major forest fire which was destined to spread much further south. Flames which began more than one hundred miles north of Porcupine Junction licked their way southward and the inferno proved to be unstoppable. Water bombers worked feverishly and the efforts of exhausted fire-fighting crews were futile in quenching the flames. The raging blaze continued and clouds of dense smoke from the forest fire drifted south on a daily basis.

As the fire ripped and roared its way through the north woods, the Gear family was one of the first to feel its effects.

When Basil Gear realized the potential danger of the approaching inferno, he'd already had several days of warning, giving the family time to load many of their personal possessions onto a wagon equipped with a trailer hitch.

He ran over to big Jim O'Connor's farm, his nearest neighbour. "Jimmy, I've got a big problem! I'm right in line with the fire, and I need some wheels to get my loaded trailer into the Junction. Can you help?"

"As soon as I gas up my Case tractor, I'll be over."

The Gears were one of the first families to be forced out by the fire but it also meant there was a wide choice of places in the Junction where they could be billeted until the blaze could be brought under control.

As the flames raced through the tinder dry forest, Myrtle Butler warned Nell. "Even though the blaze is still many miles away, unless something magical happens, we're going to be in deep trouble."

Abner Moss was the first to say. "Wouldn't it be ironic, after we've fought to preserve our way of life here in Porcupine Junction from the negative effects of technology and progress, only to have it wiped out by a catastrophe seemingly representative of the work of the Devil?"

Bert Parker, Big Jim O'Connor and Clyde Wopper stood just outside of Bert's shop. Bert gazed off into the forest and ran his hand over his scalp, ruffling his hair. "You can taste the rank odour of charred timber in the air."

Jimmy nodded in agreement, pointing towards the north. "Look at that great swirling mass over there. That's smoke, definitely not just some threatening thunder cloud." Then he shook his head and frowned. "I managed to get the Gears into town safely, but I'm afraid their place will be as badly off as mine once the fire gets to it."

In response to the fear of an impending disaster, Mildred McKay, who'd been standing just inside Bert's shop near Abner Moss, stepped up to the blackboard to scratch her own advice. "Here's something to think about," she said and wrote. *How a person masters his fate is more important than what his fate is."*

Then Myrtle Butler added her own advice on the board. *The only certainty is that nothing is certain,* and *Today's decisions are tomorrow's realities.*

Nell Parker showed up at Bert's shop with a half dozen blueberry pies and an assortment of other baked goods to help cheer up the worriers.

Bert couldn't help but ask his wife, "You recall when Klaus Barnaby offered to buy up your town site years ago? Do you wish you'd sold it to him then before this fire threat showed up?"

"No I don't, dear. Now folks have a good reason to work together. We'll beat this horrible blaze yet. You just wait and see! I've got confidence in you and the folks who live here in the Junction."

By the following morning there was no question that the blazing tongues of Hell would, in the next few days, be within striking distance of the village.

The obvious question posed by the group waiting in front of the shop was directed towards Bert."How do you propose we deal with an inferno that so far has ripped through everything in its path?"

With a wave of his hand, Bert gestured towards the blackboard's quotations. "Perhaps we should take these words of advice to heart." He then ushered the bystanders into his shop where he was about to reveal a fact about which very few villagers were aware.

"We're not dead yet folks. I'd like to let you all in on a secret about our village."

The circle of people around him was silent.

"Haven't you noticed anything unusual about the way this village is laid out? Let me point out one of its novel features."

In response to Clyde Wopper's quizzical look he continued. "Before Nell sold off residential lots and began any building fifty years ago, she sought the advice of a town planner from down south. He suggested that Nell leave five hundred feet between the bush and any planned buildings."

"And did she do that?" Jimmy O'Connor asked.

"You bet she did. There's a strip of land consisting mostly of sand extending from the sand pit near the fire hall over to one end of Moosehide Lake."

"What does that mean?" Myrtle asked.

"It provides a natural fire barrier which we've not kept free of undergrowth and it's become hidden by scrub trees which over the years have grown up obscuring the sand. Planners were very aware of the great fire of '29, and made allowances to hopefully avoid the repeat of a similar disaster."

Mildred McKay responded with, "I always knew Nell was a smart lady."

Bert continued. "What we need to do before the inferno arrives is clear out all of that scrub that's grown up on the sand break. As further protection we can get Frank Sattachi to plow furrows through that area. If he doesn't have enough fuel on hand for his old Massey Harris tractor to haul his plow, he can always use his team of Clydesdales to provide the power. Once we clear the undergrowth from that strip of land, it will provide us with some protection."

Many people nodded and Berth went on. "Joe Snell, the Acting-Fire Chief, has pumps for high pressure hoses and we have a ready water supply from Moosehide. We still have electrical power to run Joe's pumps from the underwater cable which runs under the lake." He paused for a moment and then said, "This would be a good time to appeal to Wallace Bottomley to dust off some of his organizational skills that he says he's honed during the Battle of Britain. Using his talents, and working together, I know that we can conquer this monster breathing fire at our doorstep."

"You got that right, friend," hollered Abner. ""However things don't look quite so good for Raven Lake since it's right in the path of the blaze which should hit there before it strikes us. Exit roads have been kept open to the south of Raven Lake in case they have to evacuate the town, so we may be getting an influx of refugees from Raven Lake into our village as the fire progresses further.

"That's right, Abe," Bert said, "But one problem closer to us here is the Moose Antler Reserve. When it was planned years ago, Chief Martin requested sufficient land to include a fire break around their village like ours, but short-sighted government officials wouldn't allow them to include the additional land. I've already informed the Chief that if their homes become threatened, his people are welcome to come into the Junction and we'll find spots to accommodate them here."

"We sure can," said Mildred.

"I knew I could count on you all," Bert said. "Once all threats of the fire are over, we can help them rebuild the reserve and hopefully they'll be able to come up with a newer and safer design before any rebuilding is finalized."

Shortly after Bert had disclosed the existence of the hidden fire break, he took Wallace Bottomley aside. "Wallace, how would you like to dust off your war experience and organize crews to clear the sandy strip. Frank Sattachi has plenty of fuel in his Massey Harris to plow that stretch of land which I hope will be enough of a hindrance to stop the advancing blaze."

"Sure thing Bert. I can organize the firefighting tasks and relieve you of that extra work."

To counteract the approaching fire which had been generating gale force winds from the north, Wallace spoke to his crews of volunteers. "Keep watch lads along the break to make sure the flames don't gain any foothold over the cleared out sandy fire break."

When Wallace arrived at Bert's shop, he squinted off towards the north and said, "The strength of that north wind has the potential of whipping sparks and burning twigs into the village. We'd better keep a sharp eye on that!"

Wallace's crew of designated spotters assured that any potential fire source did not gain a foothold in any of the Junction's buildings during their watch.

At night, during the weeks that Wallace faced the wall of fire, he tossed and turned trying to sleep. Nightmarish flashbacks of the raging Battle of Briton from half a century ago raced through his mind. He re-lived the image of smoking ruins, the nausea of burnt flesh and cries of victims trapped in the mounting mass of bombed out buildings.

By comparison, the Junction's collision and its potential destruction from the approaching inferno now rested solely in the hands of the village's citizenry and Wallace's unique organizational skills. He could only hope the village's survival would mirror that of London, England after its battle with attacking forces during the Second World War.

At one point Nell Parker was standing on her back porch when she heard wild shouts and a commotion coming from the Reserve. Nell's first thought was that it sounded like a war party on the attack, but then she realized that the scrambling natives were carrying buckets and ladders. Before she knew what was happening, they were on the roof of her store putting out a blaze before it could cause any major damage.

As the wall of burning timber advanced towards the village, Hector Critter, the preacher from Raven Lake ended one of his rants with, "That inferno is worse than the biblical breath of the hounds of Hell!"

Clyde Wopper who had been standing near Bert's shop chatting with other villagers was scanning the sky just beyond the reserve. As he watched flames shoot up the length of a dead pine cascading a shower of sparks into the heavens, he realized this was not the time for holding a social gab fest, but a time for action. He charged off to his school bus (if you could call his wobbling amble a charge) and yanked up the tongue of a trailer sitting nearby. He clunked the trailer's hitch onto the ball attached to the back of the bus.

He had realized the immediate danger which was threatening the nearby Algonquin Reserve. With the trailer hooked to the back of his yellow International bus, and with him behind the wheel, the old clunker charged onto the reserve property and disappeared through a dense wall of swirling smoke.

In what seemed like mere minutes, like an apparition, the bus loaded with women, children, and older lads shot back out of the cloud of smoke. Flames roared not far behind. The trailer was loaded with as many personal belongings as could be crammed into that limited amount of space. Martin Eagle Claw's pickup followed in Clyde's wake with the cab and back of the pickup filled to capacity with a collection of the remaining members of the reserve. From the waving arms and legs in the back of the chief's pickup, kids were screaming and crying as the adults tried to settle them down.

Wallace called over to Jim Butler and Huntley Carver who were standing idly nearby. "Hey, you two lads.I need you to arrange for sleeping accommodation for these folks. You can use Bert's shop and the village municipal meeting hall if you need extra space."

Soon after Clyde's charge onto the reserve, livestock began to filter in from Frank Sattachi's farm. Frank and his wife Beulah on his old Massey Harris tractor followed the animals' exodus as they urged along his Clydesdales, bawling cattle, flights of free-range chickens, a mini herd of terrified sheep, and a dozen squealing pigs.

As Frank on his old tractor rumbled past Huntley Carver, Hartley shouted up to Frank, "Have you seen anything of Weasel MacAdoo recently?"

"I headed up his way yesterday but the fire drove me back so I didn't get to see him. It doesn't look too good for the MacAdoos the way that inferno was tearing through everything in its path. I come across some of his critters wanderin' down the Fifth so I let them just tag along behind mine."

Frank was referring to half a dozen Jerseys, and two dozen sheep following in single file behind Weasel's ram Old Jeremiah. Huntley assisted Frank with herding the animals, and Frank's Border collie, Mirk, was a great help in gathering up the wandering livestock and driving the terrified animals to an enclosed area near the shore of the lake. Drinking water was thus available until the animals food supplies could be tended to.

Howard Oakley in his pickup, loaded with his wife Rosie, their three kids and all of their salvageable possessions, roared into the village. Howard hollered out through the pickup's side window, "We stayed as long as we could, but the fire was too much! The same thing just happened to Mike Merganzer. He and his family are right behind us."

To add to the confusion, a moose with a smoking patch on its haunch and a black bear with singed hide scampered through the village and plunged sizzling into Moosehide Lake. Flocks of Canada Geese heading south as well as partridges and pheasants converged out onto the spit towards the marina and into the safety of the lake.

Just when everything seemed to be settling down, there was a rumbling roar and the snapping of branches from the pall of smoke drifting up from the smouldering destruction.

Huntley Carver shielded his eyes and peered off towards the racket. "Well I'll be damned!"

From out of the devastation growled Eldon MacAdoo's tracked troop carrier with Weasel at the controls. His long neck and head poked out through the top turret and his war surplus helmet was perched at a cocky angle.

Huntley carver expressed the obvious question on everyone's mind at that point. "Where the Hell have you been all this time Weasel? We thought you were goners."

"No, we got cut off by the fire before we could get out. I filled a few crocks of water, soaked our house floor from the pump, parked Nellie in the basement and gathered what food was hanging around. We hunkered down in our cold room until the fire burned over. There was plenty to eat and drink so we weren't too badly off. Our house went up in smoke and it was a little warm where we were at times.Once the flames died down, I fired up Old Nellie. She was unscorched in the basement and ran like a charm, so here we are!"

As the forest fire progressed towards Raven Lake, Roving Reporter Mildred McKay provided full coverage. When residents were forced to evacuate the town, she was an integral part of the evacuation. She did in-depth interviews with fire-fighters Bert Parker, Wallace Bottomley and Chief Joe Snell.

Mildred knew that her job was in jeopardy due to the evacuation, but as had been the plan previously, she kept writing stories about the fire and filed them for future use once the fire was brought under control. This included any other interesting happenings which might show up on her radar, even if they weren't fire related. Although a forest fire was not something to be laughed about, Mildred was still able to peer through the smoke of a disastrous situation and brush the soot off of any humorous incident that would provide a good story.

Seeing Eldon MacAdoo navigate his tracked vehicle out of the smoking desolation of the fire was analogous to Bonsai Ben's Phoenix Cafe arising from the ashes of a catastrophe.

14

Whistling In The Wilderness

If you keep your mouth shut,
you will never put your feet in it
(Eldon MacADoo)

As the relentless fiery maelstrom continued eating its way toward the Junction, it was just after dinner when Jim Butler stepped out the kitchen doorway of the Dew Drop Inn. Like a groundhog sniffing its surroundings, Jim scratched his bald head and inhaled the sharp odour of smoke in the night air. What had been a warm breeze during the day had grown in strength as the blaze approached the Junction.

Jim strained his ears to identify a new sound. Was it his imagination or was that the screech of a steam engine's whistle? He said aloud, "That's impossible! It's been years since steam engines ran on the spur line running off the Ontario Northland's main line." He remembered when the lumber mills had been shut down on the spur section forcing railway employees to tear up the rails and cart them away for scrap metal.

He wondered if he was losing his mind? Perhaps like so many others in the Junction, the approaching blaze was straining their nerves to the breaking point. He tugged open the Inn's back door and called to Myrtle. "Will you come out here and tell me if I'm losing my sanity? Just listen and tell me if you don't hear a train whistle."

With a dish towel over her shoulder Myrt tucked in her apron and cocked a discerning ear. "I don't hear anything." She turned to head back into the kitchen but stopped abruptly. "Wait. You're right. There is a whistling noise, but it can't be a train. There are no tracks around any longer."

Jim tried to explain the sound. "Maybe its got something to do with the fire?"

The following morning he approached a group hanging around Bert's shop. "Did anybody hear what sounded like a train whistle last night?" From the puzzled blank looks he received, he expected someone to tell him he was going crazy.

But Mildred McKay piped up with, "I did!" A

discussion followed until Clyde Wopper suggested he go over and have a chat with headman Martin Eagle Claw. "Perhaps his Medicine Man, Isaac Quail Tail can offer a solution He knows about spirits and all of that stuff."

Later that day Jim tramped over to the Reserve and was gone for a good half hour before he returned to the group near Bert's shop. Huntley Carver was the first to ask. "Well Jimmy, are you any the wiser now?"

Jim liked to prolong the mystery. "Weeell, Isaac built a smoky fire, tossed in some rabbit fur, stirred the flame, made a few weird incantations and ended up saying, 'It's no train whistle. I say it's the Voice of Nature screaming in agony from the fire'."

"Maybe by the time the inferno burns itself out we'll get a true answer to the mystery."

As the blaze advanced towards the village, whenever it flared up, the whistling would intensify then fade out. Most villagers believed that the fire was becoming less intense and on the verge of dying out. It was a Monday morning when the blaze finally did drop to a dense blanket of smoke. The wailing whistle had become very fierce when the blaze closed in on the village. In a final display of the fire's power, a dead pine standing fifty feet from the blaze break burst into flame. The flames gnawed their way up the dead trunk, causing the great pine to crash to the ground. As it fell it let out a terrifying screech.

Fire Chief Joe Snell hiked through burning embers to what had once been the fallen pine's tallest point. "Well folks, there's your answer to the phantom steam engine whistle. There's a split in the top of the tree. When the winds blew through that crack it made a screeching sound like a steam engine's whistle." He put his hands on his hips. "There's a logical answer for everything it you dig down and examine the facts closely enough."

The inferno continued to chomp towards the border of Porcupine Junction and Moosehide Lake, leaving behind a forest of blackened skeletal remains attesting to the severity of the blaze. What was once an inferno was now reduced to a smouldering mass of charred timber.

After months of devastation throughout the North, tireless fire-fighting crews had tamed the roaring monster to a smoky and placid whimper. Doc Doolittle was kept busy treating burn injuries and he remained in constant contact with his son Maxwell, who was away studying immunology at the University of Montreal.

When the forest fire threatened the village of Porcupine Junction, Doc Doolittle kept re-assuring his son that the village and its residents had the challenging fire well in hand, but he didn't realize that his son was fighting a threat of his own.

15

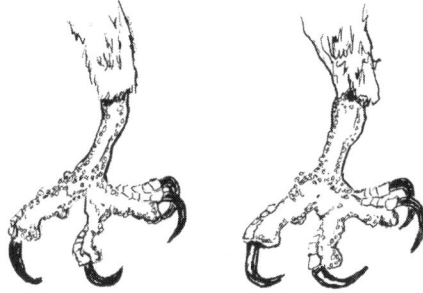

On a Wing and a Prayer

The future belongs to those alone
who can hear it.
(Billy Williams)

Early in their young lives, the Caboose kids, Charles and Helen, attended the elementary school in Raven Lake. Under the eagle eye of school bus driver Clyde Wopper, Chuckie and Little Raven made this their daily educational pilgrimage.

Charles was the most dedicated of the two when it came to educational pursuits. His main sphere of interest (particularly when he got to high school) was the study of sciences. After he graduated from elementary school, 'Chuckie' delighted in studying mathematics, physics, chemistry and particularly biology—his chief interest being in the natural sciences. One day a guidance counsellor asked, "What would you like to do Charles after you graduate from high school?"

Chuckie replied, "I'd like to go to university an' study science."

"Any special branch of science?'

"I might like to become a veterinarian specializing in birds or else I'd like to be an environmentalist." He paused and then said, "I'm not sure which one. I'll have to think more about those two possibilities more before I make up my mind."

Obviously Charles Caboose had his sights set high, but those who knew him felt that he certainly had the ability to succeed in either of these fields. One day while Charles was still in junior grades, his father brought home from the literary section of Bert Parker's Fix-It Shop a volume with the title, *Birds of Prey* by Floyd Scholz. This book got Chuckie more interested in avian studies and particularly in raptors and other such winged predators. In history class, he'd read about training hawks and eagles and he even dreamed that someday, he'd be able to train one of his own raptors.

One afternoon on the way home from high school, he stopped in at the Porcupine Quill Bookstore run by Nancy in Raven Lake and began snooping through a catalogue of books. *Falconry & Hawking by*

Phillip Glasier further fueled Chuckie's interest in one day training an eagle or hawk himself. He wrote down the name of the book and planned to ask his dad to order one from Nancy for his next birthday.

Gary Caboose once told him, "It's nice to dream, son, but we don't have eagles and hawks around Porcupine Junction so you might better be thinking about graduating from school and perhaps setting your sights on becoming a vet. Once you finsih university and become a veterinarian you might have the chance to meet people who raise birds such as hawks or eagles."

So, Charles took his father's wise advice and thought little more of his dream. Chuckie had to continue his studies of birds at home because the Raven Lake School was closed from the forest fire disaster throughout the north. While studying at home, he still harboured his dream of training his own raptor.

In pursuit of his interest in nature, Chuckie would often wander through the bush around the Junction and along the shores of Moosehide Lake. During many of those outings, Nell Parker's dog Buddy would often tag along. On one of the trips along the shore of the lake, Chuckie noticed a nest built of sticks in the crotch of a tall spruce. He could see that the nest was inhabited as he watched two adult birds come and go but he wasn't sure what breed the birds were.

Any day that an intense wind blew in from the north, faint wisps of smoke drifted down from the forest fire which was still burning, even though it was no longer a major threat. With his limited knowledge of natural science, Charles felt sure that any threat of fire would be unsettling to the wildlife around their village.

It was during a foray along the shore of Moosehide that Chuckie's life changed. Buddy's barking drew Charles to investigate something unusual near the base of the bird-nest spruce tree. Closer investigation revealed that a fledgling had fallen out of the nest. Charles knew that he had to do something quickly. "Careful Budd, you'll frighten the wee fellow. We can't leave that little bird here. It'll never survive."

Charles tucked the small featherless fledgling inside his jacket to keep warm and with Buddy in tow, they headed back towards the marina.

Gary Caboose assumed that the bird which his son had rescued was a young Osprey since that was the type that he would expect to find near a lake stocked with fish, a favourite food of such a predator.

"Can I keep him dad? We could never get him back into his nest."

"If you do, you're going to have to take good care of him, an' it'll take an awful lot of work."

Thinking about feeding the baby, Charles asked, "What do you think it will eat?"

"Since it's probably a young Osprey, I suppose minnows would be the answer."

"I'll go down to the dock and catch a few. I can keep a supply in a bucket near the house until I need them. Do you think it's a he or a she?"

"I'm not sure, but when I go to Bert's Fix-It shop tomorrow, I'll see if anyone there knows more about birds than I do."

As planned, when Gary arrived at the shop the next day, he took Bert aside and asked to address the group about his son's problem. As soon as Bert heard that Charles wanted to raise a young Osprey that he'd rescued, Bert immediately suggested, "Gary, before you speak with the group I think that you should talk to Billy Williams."

"Who?"

"William Williams, that old Welsh fellow who moved into town last summer. He lives in that little white cottage over near the fire hall."

"Why him?"

"Well, he recently emigrated here from Wales, and I understand he knows a lot about birds. I heard that he usta work with folks in Wales who raised raptors, and I think that he even spent a while workin' with a vet who ran an Avian Veterinarian practice."

"Good idea, Bert. Thanks."

"He's a bit of a strange old duck, but I think he's just the person that you need to talk to."

When Gary returned home, he told his son what he'd learned at the shop. I think you'd better head over and talk to Mr Williams as soon as you can. His house is the little white one next to Chief Joe Snell's place, over by the fire hall."

Since it was still early afternoon, Charles set out immediately and was soon knocking on Mr. Williams front door.

The age of short and pudgy William Williams, had pushed well past three score and ten at least by a half dozen years. Bill wore a Deerstalker Sherlock Holmes style hat whenever he went ambling around Porcupine Junction. He was pretty much bald except for the odd salt and pepper sprout of hair which poked out erratically from under his cap. Billy's peanut-size snout was offset by a pointy chin which stuck out between chubby cheeks over a wobbly double chin.

He usually wore a woolen walking jacket over a matching vest, and baggy woolen trousers circled his ample middle while knee-high woolen stockings kept each pant leg firmly in check. A pair of clumpy chestnut brown walking shoes complemented the rest of Bill's sartorial splendor.

When Charles arrived at the Williams residence, Billy was sitting perched on the end section of a remodeled church pew located on his front porch. The elderly gent was leaning on the pew's arm rest puffing profusely on his old briar, its bowl blackened from eons of use. Since Bill had no teeth, he had cut off the stem of his pipe and wound the remainder of the stem with black electrician's tape so he could clamp the pipe firmly in his gums. No one knew what brand Billy Williams smoked in his briar, but whatever it was, it was always wise to (always) stand well upwind whenever he had her fired up.

"Good afternoon Mr. Williams. My name is Charles Caboose, but you can call me Chuckie if you want."

"What can I do you for, son?"

"I've got a problem that I hope you can help me with. I found what I think is a baby Osprey that fell out of its nest and I'm tryin' to keep it from diein' and I wondered if you could help me out since folks say you know all about birds."

"Well, lad, I don't know ALL about birds but I'd be glad to help you out if I can. Where is this wee creature right now?"

"It's at my house inside in a box with a screen on the front. It's tucked in on the bottom of the cage sittin' on a towel to keep warm."

"You live at the Big Canoe Marina don't you?"

"That's right."

"I'll drop by tomorrow morning at about nine to see what you've gotten yourself into."

"Great! I'll be waitin." Charlie Caboose slept well that night as he anticipated a visit from Mr.

Williams the following morning.

Chuckie was outside early in the morning just as Mr. Williams turned the corner near the marina. Billy was wearing his traditional Deerstalker, clumpy walking shoes, woolen jacket and puffing as usual on his ever-present briar. With his head lowered, he peered out from under the peak of his hat. Clouds of smoke billowing out of Mr. Williams' pipe reminded Charles of a determined steam locomotive chugging up a steep grade. When he arrived at the marina doorway, Billy knocked the glowing dottle from his briar on the heel of his shoe then tucked the pipe into his jacket pocket. With a greeting of, "Good morning," Billy followed Charles through the doorway and into the marina.

When they reached the bird box, Billy opened the lid, reached inside and gently plucked out the wee bird which was just beginning to sprout a few fluffy feathers. Billy held the little creature in his thick calloused hand, tilted his head slightly, squinted through both eyes then declared, "You're right lad. What you've got here is a fine specimen of a male Pandion Haliaetus. I see you've been taking good care of him."

"What did you say he was?"

"He's a Pandion Haliaetus. That's just a five dollar word for what folks around here would call an Osprey."

"That's great! I thought you said he had some sort of disease."

"Nope, he looks to be in good shape. Has he got a name yet?"

"No, I didn't know if it was a he or she. Since it's a him, I think that I'll call him Jester. Do you think I'd ever be able to train him the way they do with eagles an' hawks?"

"Well, the short answer is 'probably yes', but you've got a long way to go before you even reach that stage. I'll drop by and take a look at him every couple of days and in case of emergency, feel free to drop by my place and between the two of us we'll do our best to see that Jester has a long and healthy contented life. Your main job right now is to make sure that he's well looked after."

The smile on Chuckie's face showed a unanimous agreement.

"Just a few words of advice though before you even think of training Jester the way many others do with their raptors. They say you'll need the patience of a Buddhist Monk and the delicate hands of a concert organist to train a raptor. It won't be an easy task, but it will be rewarding if you succeed."

Chuckie's eyes got wider and his smile broader the more William Williams spoke.

"I'll tell you more about myself and the equipment you'll need as time goes on but, first things first."

During the weeks that followed, Chuckie learned that Mr. Williams had worked as a vet's assistant at the Snowdonia Wildlife Sanctuary in Wales. They treated injured birds, raised endangered avian species by incubating their eggs and advised trainers of raptors about proper procedures to raise their charges in a healthy manner.

Billy further advised Charles."Once Jester matures to the training stage, you'll need a leather hood for him, a glove for your left hand to protect you, some leather lines, and a whistle."

"Where can I get all that stuff?" Chuckie asked.

"I believe Basil Gear just arrived in town after his family left their cabin threatened by the forest fire. I know his leather crafting is excellent so he should be able to custom create all the equipment you'll need for training Jester. So that's something to keep in mind for the future."

Chuckie's osprey education continued on a later visit from Billy. "Let me tell you a few facts about these birds that you might not be aware of. As you probably do know, they build their nests near lakes because they like to feed on fish."

Charlie nodded.

"The osprey is neither an eagle nor a hawk. It actually belongs to its own genus known as the large 'fish eagle.' The osprey flies over open water looking for swimming fish and can hover, watching its prey, then it will dive down with a splash into the water." On his last sentence, Billy's hand came swooping down with a dive.

He continued. "Its feet are the most interesting part of an osprey's anatomy. They are heavily scaled and are fitted with spiny projections called spicules on its feet pads, ideal for holding onto fish. It also has the ability to swivel its toes to grip its quarry. This allows the osprey to fly while holding onto its prey. It can thus point a captive fish in the direction in which the osprey is flying and thereby reduce the wind resistance. Their long pointed wings are ideal for allowing them to lift very heavy loads such as large fish or marine animals that they've caught."

"Do you think I'll be able to train Jester?" Chuckie asked.

"I don't know of anyone who has ever trained an osprey like they do raptors, so if you manage to do so, you'd likely be one of the first."

"How big will Jester get?"

"A fully mature osprey stands about two feet tall and females are usually larger than the males. Both are for the most part white breasted, with blue-gray legs and adults have bright yellow eyes with a distinctive brown eye stripe."

Billy Williams' visits to the marina and Chuckie's meticulous care paid dividends so that Jester soon reached maturity. With his increase in size, Charles convinced his father to allow him to house his new pet in one of the marina's larger rooms which at the time was vacant. Charles built several perches in the room and made sure that there was always a supply of water available.

Jester's flying ability improved and he was able to fly from perch to perch in the enlarged space. The day finally arrived when Billy suggested, "Okay my boy I think it's about time we started on this training business. The first thing we need is a hood for Jester and a leather glove for your left hand along with a set of leather straps, or jesses to attach to Jasper's legs. To these jesses we will attached a cord or creance which will allow Jester to fly, but he'll still be attached to you."

Charlie had been avidly studying the book *Falconry & Hawking* that his father had bought him for his birthday. In it were a good many patterns for leather equipment that he'd need.

Billy continued. "The leather hood I was talking to you about is intended to deceive the bird making it think it's dark out or night-time when raptors are most relaxed. That's where the term 'hoodwinked' comes from."

A week later, Basil Gear delivered a newly crafted leather hood for Jester, a glove for Charlie's left hand and some leather lines.

On Billy's next visit, Charlie excitedly asked him, "Where do I start?"

Bill looked at the new equipment, nodding his head. "One of the first steps in training a raptor is called manning. You need to encourage Jester to hop from his perch onto your gloved fist and then you'll have to spend hours walking around as you two become trusting and comfortable with each other. Likely you can see now why they say you need the patience of a Buddhist Monk if you plan to train a raptor."

It was not unusual from that day on for folks in the village to encounter Charles at all hours of the day walking with his osprey (usually on his gloved fist), but once in a while Chuckie would allow Jester to ride along perched on his shoulder.

During one of his visits to Bert Parker's Fix-It Shop, Bert said to Gary, "Would you ask Charles to drop by the shop with Jester. A lot of the folks in the village are curious seeing the pair of them walking around town. Tomorrow morning would be a great time if it's convenient to the two of them."

As requested, the next morning, with Jester poised proudly on his gloved fist, and with Helen behind lugging a portable perch, Charles entered Bert's Shop. They settled in the work area, and Charles pointed and asked Helen, "Set up the perch over there, about ten feet away, and I'll see if I can get Jester to cooperate."

Charles sat Jester on the perch then walked back the full length of the creance attached to Jester's jesses. Chuckie took out a whistle, blew three sharp notes and held up his gloved fist. Jester leapt from the perch and swooped over to the proffered gloved hand. Charles then rewarded Jester with a small piece of trout which he extricated from a pouch strapped to his waist.

When that feat went as planned in front of all of those spectators, there was no one prouder than Charles Caboose. He received a big round of applause from the intrigued villagers who had gathered to watch the display. What Charles had just demonstrated was one of the first steps to be mastered before a raptor could eventually be released and allowed to fly freely in the hope that it would return on cue.

One of the concerns in training a raptor is to be conscious of its weight. The bird should be properly fed so that it is kept nourished but always slightly hungry. An overweight bird is not what owners want in a raptor destined to hunt.

As a gift, Bert Parker presented Charles with a set of scales that he'd originally purchased as a birthday present for Nell to aid in her cooking measurements. But Nell advised her husband, "I don't need any such fancy gizmo like that to help with my cooking. A dab of this, and a pinch of that, is good enough for me. Your fancy scales would probably mess up my results."

Following his wife's objections, Bert decided to present the scales to Charles for weighing his bird.

At one stage in Jester's weighing, Charles became concerned because his pet's weight seemed to be falling. When he expressed his concern to Billy Williams, the old man made an unusual request. "Let me have a look at his droppings in the room where he spends the night." After making his inspection, Billy made his diagnosis, "I think he's got the beginning of an infection. I know how we used to treat the problem back home, but I don't know what would be the equivalent drug to use over here. We'll have to talk it over with Doctor Doolittle to see what he thinks."

Doc Doolittle didn't react too kindly to Billy's request. "Do you expect me to treat a bird? I'm a people doctor, not a vet!"

Bill continued. "Calm down Doc. All I'm asking for is a little advice. I'll tell you the name of the antibiotic I used in Wales, and I'd like to know what the equivalent might be over here."

"Oh. Alright, if that's all you want to know, but I don't want word of this to get out to any of my regular patients or they'll think they're being treated by a vet and not an actual doctor."

"Don't worry. This will be kept between the four of us: me, you, Charles, and Jester."

After that, Charles obtained from Wallace's pharmacy the comparable drug suggested by Doc Doolittle. It did the job and Jester was soon back on the mend.

In addition to training Jester to respond to a whistle, Charles also used a lure which was tied to the end of a six-foot line. The whirling lure when spun around his head was intended to represent a swimming fish. Charles allowed Jester to fly freely in one of his father's storage barns and he flew Jester on longer and longer creance lines until he was convinced that if given his complete freedom, Jester would return in response to the whistle and lure.

As is the case with all trainers of raptors, during the first test of free flight, there is always a sense of perspiration until the bird returns on cue to receive its reward of food.

Charles was no exception. He unhooked the restraining line from Jester's jesses and with a wave of his gloved fist allowed Jester to climb unrestrained into the sky. Charles watched Jester climb upwards, circle overhead, then glide across the surface of

Moosehide Lake. Now would come the moment of truth following all of Jester's training.

Since Charles decided that Jester's short flight was sufficient, he blew three blasts on the whistle and spun the lure through several rotations around his head and waited . . . hoping. After approximately three minutes, Jester swooped down and landed on Charles' gloved fist. Charles breathed a sigh of relief at Jester's successful return and was glad to hand over a choice morsel of trout that the bird had been expecting.

Following that first successful free flight, not all of Jester's releases went quite as flawlessly. After one period of free flight when Jester did not return as expected, Charles was in a panic. His immediate reaction was to contact Billy Williams to explain that Jester had failed to return. Billy was not quite so concerned and explained to Charles. "Since you let him free late in the afternoon, go home and return to the same spot the next morning. By then Jester will have been out all night and probably will be getting hungry. If you blow your whistle and try to recall him then, it's likely that he will respond.

Charles had no choice but to do as Billy suggested. Sure enough, after Charles had spent a sleepless night, he returned the next morning with his whistle and lure, and Jester appeared out of the blue as if he'd never been free on his own all night.

This was the first of several wrinkles which occurred in Jester's training flights. Due to the advancing forest fire, Raven Lake had been evacuated and many of its residents ended up billeted in the Junction. All hands that were available in Porcupine Junction worked under the direction of Fire Chief Joe Snell, Bert, and Wallace Bottomley to do what they could to battle the blaze threatening the Junction.

During the time Charles did what he could to assist the fire-fighting efforts, but with school in Raven Lake suspended, Charles had plenty of time to work with Jester. Another time when Jester was flying free and had not returned as expected, Charles circulated around the village blowing his whistle and whirling the lure about his head. He was two blocks from the village fire hall when he heard another whistle. He followed the sound towards the hall where he found the volunteer firemen out on manoeuvres under the direction of the Chief. Joe Snell's whistle was intended to control the actions of his fire crew. When Charles got close to the hall, he noticed Jester perched on the top rung of the fire truck's extended ladder. Jester was waiting expectantly for the next whistle blast, probably wondering when he would get his reward of trout for returning. Charles waited for a lull in the Department's training, then blew his whistle, spun the lure around his head and as he had hoped Jester zoomed back to his gloved fist.

Due to the nearness of the blaze to the Junction, Charles confined Jester's flights to an area closer to Moosehide Lake. He even took Jester out in one of his father's canoes and released the bird over the water. It was a surprise to Charles after one free flight when he saw Jester returning, gripping a bass with a fishing lure dangling from its jaw. Chuckie learned later that one of the lads from the Reserve had been out fishing when an osprey appeared out of the blue and snatched his catch out of mid air before it landed in the bottom of the canoe. Charles sheepishly returned the lure to the surprised fisherman and explained that the incident was really his fault. Following Jester's return, Charles thought it only fair that after he had removed the lure from the bass that he allow Jester to consume a chunk of the fish as his reward for returning from his flight.

Charles found it hard to believe that Jester could have a sense of humour, but another free flight incident seemed to indicate this to be the case. It demonstrated just how true his name actually depicted his character.

Gary Caboose had been out on one of his early morning fishing expeditions and returned with his usual full limit of caught fish. As was also his custom, when Gary arrived at the dock, he handed his string of fish to his wife Yellow Feather for cleaning where she would take the fresh catch out to a cleaning table behind the Marina. After her usual fine job of cleaning and filleting, Yellow Feather would then lay the fillets out carefully according to size on the table.

On this particular occasion, after cleaning the fish, she went inside to wash her hand and when she returned to the cleaning table discovered that the largest of the fillets had mysteriously disappeared during her absence. And on that same day, when Jester returned from the latest free flight with a neatly filleted fish in his grip, Charles had seen enough of his mother's filleting to suspect where Jester's catch had come from. He did not have the nerve to confess to his mother what had probably happened, even at dinner as she described to her husband the mysterious disappearance of the fillet.

During the period that Charles had been training Jester, residents had been evacuated from Raven Lake and many of them were now housed in Porcupine Junction. School as Charles had previously known it was obviously no longer operating in Raven Lake because of the fire. Some of its teachers had settled in the Junction but Charles was still able to complete his education, of sorts, but on a much different basis. He continued his academic studies through an extensive reading program based on the vast selection in the library housed in Bert's Fix-It Shop.

However, a more personal concern was a future one which Charles would face once the fire had been brought under control. He would eventually receive his graduation diploma from the Raven Lake High School, and submit his application to attend a university down south. This would, of course, entail a move away from Porcupine Junction.

He expressed this concern to his old partner. "Bill, I can't take Jester down south when I go off to university, what will happen to him?"

In his usual logical fashion, Billy Williams had already considered this eventuality. "You've given Jester a good life lad, and treated him well. If it hadn't been for your efforts, he probably would never have survived at all. No matter what your relationship is or was with Jester, he is still a wild creature and deserves to be free."

Charles nodded gravely.

Billy continued. "I've made a few trips down to Moosehide while you were busy studying and I noticed there is a new young female osprey that has recently hatched from the pair which still inhabits the nest which Jester fell from." He stopped talking to give Charles a moment, then he said slowly, "I believe if you release Jester, he would fare well and not be alone for long."

Charles took a deep breath and straightened his shoulders with a sigh. "I was afraid this day would come."

'I know it's hard son, and not something you want to do, but for Jester's sake, it would be the wisest."

The week before Charles left the Junction, as Bill stood by his side, he removed Jester's hood, unfastened the jesses from his legs and with a wave of his gloved hand, launched Jester to his freedom.

The osprey climbed swiftly, momentarily disappearing into a cloud bank and just before he reappeared, Bill couldn't help but notice the tears that rolled down the young lad's cheek.

However, when the bird veered towards Moosehide Lake, a broad grin on Chuck's face replaced all signs of sadness. They both knew that waiting there was a young female osprey and a potential new life for the freed bird.

16

The Four Horsemen of the Apocalypse

There is no such thing in life
as an unimportant day.
(Maxwell Doolittle)

During the months of struggle, while the residents of the Junction focused on the disastrous forest fire, Doctor Maxwell Doolittle from his immunology laboratory in Montreal didn't want to worry his father that the rest of the world was becoming involved with a challenge of its own.

Maxwell reminded everyone who would listen that The Black Death was a historic pandemic dating back to the Middle Ages, and since then SARS, AIDS, Ebola and ZIKA were more recent viral crises as were swine and bird flues; any of these could become global.

Dr. Doolittle and his colleagues in the Montreal University immunology lab were at the time seeking a drug to counteract a new pandemic which had originated in Outer Mongolia. A group of archaeologists had opened an ancient tomb, where they discovered the wizened bodies of a Mongol tribal leader along with those of his many wives and children. All casualties appeared to have died from a disease which scientists were unable to identify.

Shortly after the tomb's opening, members of the archaeological team began to die off for some unexplained reason. Examination of the mysterious virus found in the tomb was unidentified, but scientists suspected that a killer gene had mutated with a disease which had been killing camels in the area. No drugs available seemed to be able to subdue the disease or contain its spreading.

Anyone infected with the new crippling scourge began to experience breathing problems, then their eyes bulged out as if from some internal pressure. Following those symptoms, victims would develop a purple skin rash, then cease breathing entirely. (All within a very short period of time.)

Due to the extent that the world's population

has been increasing exponentially, some pessimistic 'Four Horsemen of the Apocalypse' groups were predicting that a worldwide famine destined to overcome the globe would be controlled by just such a Mongol initiated pandemic. According to them, this was God's way of dealing with the potential famine resulting from the world's predicted overpopulation.

Hector Critter was among a group of Religious Fanatics who were quick to describe the pandemic to the public as *Dromedary Black Death*. Immunologists had not yet discovered a vaccine to counteract this disease, so they continued to identify the killer strain of virus by its scientific name, IMOXY-DD-XIII.

Dr. Maxwell Doolittle was one of those in the forefront closest to achieving a breakthrough in eradicating the disease.

Following the pandemic's emergence in Outer Mongolia, it next broke out in the Chinese capital, continued through that country and then into Asia and the Middle East. Due to the facility of air travel and the lack of proper health precautions, pockets of *Dromedary Black Death* began to show up in Europe and soon thereafter in North and South America.

During the months that the forest fires raged through the north and threatened Porcupine Junction, the *Dromedary Death world-threatening pandemic* had been killing off the world's population. For Porcupine Junction the forest fire was a blessing in disguise. The inferno's threat on The Junction isolated the village from physical contact with the rest of the world.

There was even a case of Angela Howzer, a young lady from Raven Lake who returned from visiting her son, a helicopter pilot in Dubai. Angela, through her travels, unknowingly brought the disease closer to Porcupine Junction.

When the pandemic gained a foothold in Raven Lake, flames annihilated the Black Dromedary Death spores which might have had any chance of being carried by the wind and infecting the Junction.

As the pandemic raged around the globe, steadily reducing the planet's population, Maxwell Doolittle's team continued to work on in his laboratory in Montreal in search of the key to combat the epidemic.

Angela, who succumbed to the disease in Raven Lake was the young lady to whom Maxwell Doolittle had proposed one year previous to the emergence of the killing virus. The wedding was to have taken place when the doctor returned to Porcupine Junction after his contract in Montreal had expired.

It was approximately two months after the end of the fire threat to Porcupine Junction that Maxwell Doolittle's team finally achieved conclusively the key for which they had been searching to stop and ultimately eliminate the Dromedary Death. Following the death of Angela Howzer, for Maxwell, his team's success was a bittersweet moment. When he learned of Angela's death, it had inspired Maxwell and his team to work harder to conquer the pandemic and prevent it from killing other innocent people.

When the world at large learned of the pandemic's cure by Doolittle's team, they also became aware of the existence of the tiny northern village of Porcupine Junction. They learned how the village had never become infected by the plague and of its connection with Dr. Maxwell Doolittle. Through the media of newspapers and television, word also spread about the existence of Bert's Fix-It Shop and how world affairs were discussed by an unlikely group of seniors who met in the shop on a regular basis.

As word of Porcupine Junction, and the laudable values espoused by Bert Parker and his cadre of cronies spread, the village began to be compared to Utopia, the mythical name created by Sir Thomas Moore in his 1516 book *Utopia* which described a fictional idealistic society in the Atlantic Ocean.

On the other hand, some environmentalists likened Porcupine Junction to a modern-day Shangri-La like the one hidden in the Tibetan mountains and described by James Hilton in his novel *Lost Horizon*.

Considering the chaos existing in the world following the threat of Dromedary Death, the sad condition of the world's environment and general malaise of the world's population towards one another, groups began to surface with the hope of changing the world's attitude towards what was taking place in our badly fractured planet.

Bert's Fix-It Shop in Porcupine Junction became an inspiration for change necessary to fix the earth's shattered environment and examine a new sense of values. It was during this time that efforts escalated, focusing on change and the establishment of a Worldwide Movement for Environmental Rights.

Although the world threatening pandemic, Dromedary Death, took place outside Porcupine Junction, reporter Mildred McKay covered the story, focusing on the work of young Dr. Doolittle and how the pandemic did not impact Porcupine Junction.

One thing about writing a weekly column for the *Suppository News* was that Mildred found herself becoming more observant about life. It was also challenging to find something humorous about a pandemic. But, if she worked at it, she always found a kernel hidden in even the most dire incident.

17

It Ain't Over 'Til It's Over

A man is not old until regrets
take the place of dreams.
(Bert Parker)

The sun was just climbing over the horizon as Nell sat in her favourite rocker on the front porch of her General Store and Post Office. She inhaled the freshness of the north-country breezes as the morning panorama over Moosehide unfolded as it had been doing for years. The morning sun had risen as an almost perfect golden globe casting shimmers of its flaming radiance onto low hanging cumulus clouds.

Old Buddy as usual had flopped down snoozing on the deck, oblivious of the celestial grandeur unfolding around him. It was then that Nell noticed the frosty whiteness of fuzz on her companion's muzzle. Buddy's whiskers twitched as if in response to some mysterious sense by which he realized that his master was pondering his future. Nell mused aloud on what lay ahead. "Well, Old Budd, it looks as though you, Bert and I are all getting somewhat 'long-in-the-tooth.' I wonder what will happen to our village when Bert and I are no longer around to manage the reins?"

Even with her many other tasks related to operating her store and post office, Nell always found time to continue with her love of cooking. Baking her fabulous pies, kneading the latest batch of bread along with her other culinary tasks were times when Nell became lost in dreams of her past. What would life be without time spent in her kitchen? This brought to mind the quotation which she had mounted on a plaque on the wall near her kitchen stove: *Always try to inject a few raisins into the tasteless dough of life.*

Nell was not one to worry about her legacy. She and Bert had lived productive lives of which they were both proud, but from time to time, she did   wonder what would become of her store and the rest of the village once she and Bert were no longer around.

Nell's thoughts about the village's future took an unexpected turn following her receipt of a phone call from a person from the past. While bustling about in her kitchen, after pulling the last two mouth-watering blueberry pies from her oven, Nell paused to answer her ringing phone.

"Good morning, Nell Parker here!"

"Good morning, Nell. Its Klaus Barnaby here. Perhaps you may not remember me. It's been a few years."

"How could I not remember someone who once told me I was nuts because I wouldn't sell you my fifty acres of land?"

"Perhaps it's time I apologized for that. I've been hearing about your village in the news lately and I'm impressed with how The Junction has evolved since my first discussion with you those many years ago."

Nell didn't speak and Klaus continued. "It turns out that you made the right decision to turn down my offer. It's great to hear there's at least one spot on the face of our planet where common sense and concern for others reigns supreme."

"So you've finally come to your senses," she said.

He laughed. "Not only that, I've managed to accumulate a fair bit of cash during my years of involvement in the lumber business and I've become somewhat of a philanthropist lately." He paused. "I would like to make an offer which I hope you and Bert will seriously consider."

"What's that?"

"Some folks might say that in my old age my brain has become addled and that I'm just concerned about my legacy, but, as you said, I'd like to think that I've finally come to my senses."

Nell didn't say anything.

"It appears that over the years, a great many fruitful ideas have come out of the groups meeting in Bert's Fix-It Shop. Those who spent time generating ideas in Bert's shop may not have been the greatest minds in the world but I've never heard of a group of folks who could come up with so many common sense thoughts that the world should be paying more attention to, now that our planet is in such a mess."

"I have to agree with you there," Nell said.

"Well, since I'm not getting any younger, and before I cash in my chips, I'd like to do something with my life that would benefit mankind." He paused for only a short moment. "I would like to provide a grant to the village of Porcupine Junction to create a Think Tank based on the concepts espoused by the group which Bert encouraged."

"That is generous of you Klaus. Bert will be pleased."

"I'll leave it up to him and his cronies to come up with a suitable administrative plan but I would hope that he'll take me up on my offer. I'd like to upgrade his shop with more meeting and office spaces for the newly created world class Think Tank."

"A Think Tank. I would never have guessed," said Nell.

"Perhaps you would inform Bert of my offer and have him contact me so we can arrange a meeting to discuss the project."

"I will do that, Klaus."

"And I would also be interested in funding a village retirement home connected to a first rate state-of-the-art medical research facility. I've already floated the ideas past Doctors Oliver and Maxwell Doolittle. They both agreed to help me develop my plans to bring them to fruition."

When Nell hung up the phone, she sat down and shook her head. "I guess those old codgers had something to say after all."

18

Who Would'a Thunk it?

My wife has a speech impediment.
Every now and then, she stops to take a breath.
(Huntley Carver)

As soon as Nell informed Bert about Klaus Barnaby's offer, Bert passed the news along to the group meeting at the time in his Fix-It Shop. They agreed to invite Klaus to a meeting the following week in Bert's shop to discuss his offer.

When Klaus arrived for the meeting, he was surprised at the size of the enthusiastic reception committee. Bert had made it clear that he and Nell didn't expect to live indefinitely, so whatever decisions were made would eventually involve other residents of the village. To Klaus this seemed like a reasonable explanation to account for the size of the mob in attendance.

When the meeting ended, plans evolved to proceed with renovations to the shop to increase its usable space. They added a limited number of living spaces for visitors from outside the village who wished to attend any discussions in progress.

Klaus arranged to meet the Doolittles to discuss details of establishing a retirement home with attached medical research facility with Maxwell Doolittle as its administrative head.

The philanthropist invited the operators and owners of the Dew Drop Inn to a separate discussion to consider the inn becoming a literary centre catering to established and novice writers. It was to be renamed *The Inspiration Inn* and grants would be made available with an emphasis on supporting emerging authors.

Klaus also invited headman Martin Eagle Claw of the Moose Antler Reserve to a meeting to consider the development of an aboriginal meeting place built around their Antler longhouse facility. Its purpose would be to act as a museum displaying native artifacts contributed by all native bands including members of the northern Inuit. The focus of the Moose Antler complex would be on providing the opportunity to enhance native culture and preserve native languages which were rapidly disappearing around the world.

Consideration included tribes from the Amazon and representation from African groups such as those in the Kalahari Desert.

The final aspect of Klaus Barnaby's multi-pronged proposal was to meet with Benedict Hong to design a structure to house an activity centre for seniors. The focus would be on tai chi, yoga, some martial arts and general exercise, and any such related activities which would fall under the umbrella of physical wellbeing of all residents of Porcupine Junction.

Since the results would cause the tiny village to stretch its limits, one of the first think-tank topics was expansion plans. There was a general consensus expressed to retain its small town attributes. Organizers invited Jane Jacobs, the author of many books, and expert on community living to provide advice on the village's expansion. Although the outer limits of the village would be increased, all proposed facilities would remain within walking distance for all residents.

When Klaus Barnaby made his philanthropic proposal to the village of Porcupine Junction, roving reporter Mildred McKay interviewed Klaus and wrote an in-depth story for the *Suppository News* about the details of his proposal and its potential impact on the village. She even offered to conduct a reporting clinic when the Dew Drop Inn was converted into a writers' retreat.

As Mildred watched the lives of Nell and Bert ebb and flow as they aged, she realized her life too would eventually end some day as well. She wondered, "What have I accomplished in my life?" Giving it some thought, she felt that over the years she had brought enough smiles to the readers of the News to guarantee her a place in the annals of history. As long as copies of the paper existed, (even if it was in archives), her contributions would never be forgotten.

19

In The Wake of Change

You can't ever step
into the same river twice.
(Benedict Hong)

It took approximately five years for the innovative building plans to be close to completion in Porcupine Junction. At that time, Nell and Bert were still healthy and active octogenarians. Nell had been in touch with her niece Eunice and husband Walter and offered them one of the village's bungalows in which they could take up residence. Eunice worked with Nell to learn the idiosyncrasies of operating the general store and post office. This included becoming the custodian for many of Nell's unique baking recipes.

Walter was not as handy mechanically as Bert, but he was eager to learn and soon mastered the mysteries of operating the hardware end of the store's business. Walter also became a valuable member contributing to the Think Tank discussion sessions.

With the operations of their businesses in good hands, it did not take much to convince Nell and Bert to take up residence in the evolving Golden Dawn, the village's new retirement home. The Parkers' new lodging consisted of a small two bedroom apartment equipped with conveniences for cooking and entertainment. Even though they lived in the Golden Dawn, both Nell and Bert continued to come and go at will as they participated in regular village activities. Nell worked on a regular basis in her store's kitchen while Bert seldom missed discussion sessions in his shop.

It was a sad day in the village with the passing of Bert and Nell. As is often the case, with married couples, two weeks after Nell's demise, Bert's death followed. Although they did not survive to view the culmination of their revitalized village, the process was well enough advanced that they departed this earthly pale with the feeling that all of their life's work was being left in good hands.

The Parkers left instructions that following either of their deaths it was to be a time during which no tears were to be shed. In their wills they had set aside sufficient funds to bankroll wakes of the first order.

Since the couple had died within two weeks of one another, it was decided that one gigantic wake would be the way to celebrate the passing of the pair. The organization of the event was left in the capable hands of Tommy Coombs, the lawyer who served as executor of the Parkers' wills.

Tommy's first task was to decide on a venue for the wake. Since Bert's fix-it shop and the newly enhanced municipal hall were within easy walking distance of one another, Tom decided to let the wake's activities flow between these two as events dictated.

Benedict Hong's Cafe took up the challenge of catering for the event. Ben provided luncheons in both the shop and municipal offices. The availability of a quantity of liquid refreshments ensured that the wake would not be not an entirely sombre or for that matter, overly sober celebration. Spirits from Ireland made up the bulk of the liquid portion of the refreshments, but there was also an ample quantity of tea and coffee to help prevent over indulgence in alcoholic brews from getting out of hand. In spite of the availability of potent brews, participants respected the occasion enough to not let their enthusiasm reach a stage of complete inebriation. All were determined to celebrate the Parkers' lives by having fun, but not becoming obnoxious through intoxication.

Considering the availability of alcohol, one

guest made the comment, "I thought Nell was a teetotaler?"

Myrtle clarified the questioner's concern. "That was many years ago, before she discovered that a healthy slug of brandy did wonders for her lumbago."

What would an Irish Wake be without music? As was the case with other community events, there was no shortage of volunteers to man banjos, fiddles, guitars, a couple of accordions and a trio of harmonicas. There was even an Algonquin lad Ivan Potlach who contributed to the percussion section by bringing along his own set of native drums.

Dancing was rampant wherever a group settled in to perform a musical set. Square dancing mixed with line dancing, step dancing and every type of dancing with perhaps the exception of ballet. It was amazing how such a variety of tunes could breathe life into dancing shoes, many of which were assumed to have atrophied with age. Perhaps these were ones fueled by alcohol?

As the day was settling in and the wake's revellers were close to exhaustion, in the early evening a gentleman showed up to cap off the day's activities. Lorne Blackson was a slender octogenarian with slicked back locks and an impressive matching salt-and-pepper handlebar moustache. Lorne was an ex-Roman Catholic cleric who had departed from a career as a priest to seek one of matrimony instead. He described how he and

Bert had become friends. "We met half a century earlier while studying down south just after I entered the priesthood and Bert was completing a course in diesel mechanics. During those early years, we both had been exposed to the teachings of media guru Marshal McLuhan. During one lecture with McLuhan we watched with awe as he smoked a cigarette in class. We and other students watched in fascination waiting for the growing cigarette ash to fall onto McLuhan's Harris Tweed jacket. It is probably a result of being exposed to McLuhan's wit and wisdom that Bert had adopted such a novel way of life and encouraged the discussion groups which evolved in his Fix-It Shop."

Lorne frequently regaled friends with stories from Bert's past in the game of hockey. "He was known as 'Bert the Bouncer' whose elbows flailed whenever a puck entered a corner. Bert's overactive elbows would even have put a star hockey player such as Gordie Howe to shame. I must confess that my own slightly off-centre proboscis was a result of just such an encounter with the elbows of an over-zealous Bert in one of the corners."

At an arranged memorial session in Bert's Shop Lorne extolled the many virtues of the Parkers and praised their contributions to the community and others. He then introduced Chief Martin Eagle Claw's son, White Cloud, to say a few words on behalf of the Algonquin elders of the Moose Antler Reserve.

With a fluffy cluster of Snowy owl feathers around his neck, White Cloud`s coal-black hair appeared like a mountain poking through a bank of cumulus clouds. White Cloud announced, "In recognition of the Parkers' contributions to the native community, Bert and Nell had been granted the titles of Honorary Grand Algonquin Leaders of the Moose Antler Nation."

The morning following the wake, Lorne Blackstone and the select villagers, whose foggy heads had cleared sufficiently after the previous day's celebration, paid a visit to the Parkers' resting place in the nearby Green Acres Cemetery. On a slab of local granite marking their interment site, a stone mason had carved the words:

Here lie two visionaries

"Our lives have passed,
We sought to Inspire you all to the very last,
Weep not for us, but courage take,
In respecting each other for our sake,
For those you love never go away,
They walk beside you every day."

Ex-reverend Blackson paused in front of the memorial for a moment. He read the inscription aloud, then blessed the couple for all they'd done for the world and for Porcupine Junction in particular. The few Porcupiners who had accompanied Lorne and his wife Mary to the cemetery lingered on the site taking the occasion to relive stories about The Parkers and events they'd experienced in their rich lives. The Blacksons then departed from the Junction and headed back to their hometown on the shore of Lake Massiwippi.

Members of the lingering group suggested that authors housed in the Inspiration Inn should consider compiling a biography to commemorate the lives of the Parkers. This could be done while resource folk were still available who could fill in the blanks in Nell and Bert's rich lives before memories of those who knew them drifted away in life's shifting sands of time.

Following the demise of Nell and Bert Parker, reporter Mildred McKay did a detailed story which appeared in the obituary section of the *Suppository News*. She elaborated on the impact that the deaths would have on the future of the Junction and made sure that she'd included ample coverage of the Parkers' wake. She also interviewed Lorne and Mary Blackson and did a separate story of his life and times and previous involvement with Bert and media guru Marshall McLuhan.

Mildred felt that her greatest accomplishment was in convincing Archibald Pryor to accompany her to a presentation she made at the newly christened

Inspiration Inn where she spoke to burgeoning scribblers. Her boss even managed to smile twice, but what surprised Mildred most was when he actually told a joke (even though it was somewhat lame with a punch line involving the actions of a step-dancer with a broken leg). It was perhaps not the funniest punch-line of any comedian, but at least The Chief had changed during Mildred's employ.

20

The Final Word

The physician can bury his mistakes, but the architect
can only advise his client to plant vines.
(Lorne Blackson)

Six months after the Parkers' wake, workers completed the final finishing touches on all of the structures which were set out in Klaus Barnaby's master rebuilding plan for Porcupine Junction. Since word about the innovative community had spread world-wide, a number of highly qualified experts in a variety of fields were eager to appear at the various venues. Bert's Fix-It Shop had been renamed THE PROBE and was already advertising a list of topics up for discussion. The Golden Dawn subsidized by the

Barnaby Foundation, was well on its way to becoming known as a first rate retirement home. The Dew Drop Inn, which had been newly christened as The Inspiration Inn, flourished and the Moose Antler Longhouse—simply called The Longhouse—was bursting with collections of native artifacts. It attracted native speakers who offered courses in dialects, some of which folks never realized existed. THE PROBE, (some folks still thought of it as Bert's Fix-It Shop) retained the blackboard on which inspirational quotations could be written while future PROBE discussion brainstorming topics were listed on a separate board. Some of these already scheduled for discussion were:

McLuhan's Global village
How the Medium Affects the Message
The Establishment of an Environmental Rights
    Movement
Lateral Thinking and Probes to Enhance
    Thinking Skills
Effects of Technology on the Human Brain

In order to promote the activities taking place in THE PROBE Think Tank, Clyde Wopper, Abner Moss and Mildred McKay collected sayings to be stenciled on multi-coloured T-shirts. Funds earned from shirt sale in the Think Tank tuck shop were channelled towards activities in that facility. Clyde`s contributions to the sayings included:

Thank God I'm An Atheist!
Anyone Who Would Go To A Psychoanalyst Should Have his Head Examined
I'm Not an Optical Illusion, I Just Look Like One
Don't Say Whoa In A Mud Hole
Always Drink Upstream From The Herd

Mildred McKay contributed the following witticisms:

Don't Talk To Me While I'm Interrupting
How Is It That Little Children Are So Intelligent, and Men Stupid? It Must Education That Does It
All I Need to Know Is How Much Is Enough,
The Best Vitamin For Making Friends Is B1
The Day Will Happen Whether Or Not You get up

At the entrance to THE PROBE, the last saying on the blackboard lingered from the Bert Parker era :

Human knowledge is always limited but human ignorance is forever boundless.

One can't help but wonder, considering the horrible state the world is in these days, and what we have experienced during our lives, if by some trick of fate we could press a reset button and return our lives to the dawn of civilization, would we have learned or would we repeat most of our mistakes all over again? It would be comforting if mankind would adopt some of the philosophies as espoused by inhabitants of the idyllic village of Porcupine Junction as visited in this novel.

And as Howard Oakley,wrote on the blackboard just inside Bert's shop, always remember:

"It's the environment stupid!!

Mac, A Mini-Biography

William Clare McCarthy (aka Mac) was born at home on April 19, 1939 in the Northern Ontario hamlet of Gold Centre. The house where he was born contained a general store operated by his mother, and was the only business in town.

In 1945, the family (parents plus five boys and two girls) moved two miles further north to Schumacher, then five years later—like the TV family The Beverly Hillbillies—the clan skedaddled south to Dunnville located on the Grand River near its mouth on Lake Erie.

Clare completed most of his public elementary and secondary schooling in Dunnville and after completing studies at Dunnville High School in 1957, he spent four years at Oueen's University in Kingston, graduating with a Specialist Degree in Mathematics. He then attended two summers qualifying to be a high school mathematics teacher.

He taught for one year in London, Ontario, three in Brampton, and thirty years in Orangeville. He served as Mathematics Department Head during much of his time in Orangeville, and he was also head of the combined math and science departments during part of that time. His subject was mathematics, but from time to time he did teach a few junior art classes.

Between 1967 and 2014, approximately 1,000 of Clare's editorial cartoons were featured in the Orangeville Banner Newspaper. Following his retirement from teaching in 1995, he began submitting a monthly column entitled *Meandering Through Life* for the Banner and in 2016 the Banner editor asked him to provide an additional column each month.

During Clare's assorted activities, he was a member of the Orangeville Art Group, President of the Orangeville Camera club and is presently Treasurer of the Headwaters Writers Guild. In 2015, Clare donated his extensive historic collection of original Banner editorial cartoons to the Dufferin county Museum and Archives.

Clare's writing career began when he retired from teaching in 1995. His first book titled *The Hurleyville Taxi* was published by Moose Hide Press in Sault Ste Marie. A second book, *Meandering,* (a collection of Banner columns) was self-published. His third book, *The Ramblings of a Curious Man,* (also self-published), was a personal memoir. He provided illustrative pen and ink drawings for all of these publications.

Clare's writing frequently leans towards a humorous bent. His literary idols include Stephen Leacock and the late newspaperman Greg Clark. Clare considers his Banner submissions to be feature writing in which he looks for what newsman Val Sears referred to as oblique bits of stories, not only the anecdotes, but the ironies.

In addition to writing his Banner columns, Clare continue to attend writing workshops to improve his skills. He belongs to the Dufferin Circle of Storytellers, part of which entails visiting Dufferin Oaks Retirement Home in Shelburne where he entertains residents with stories, and encourages them to relate stories of their own. He is presently in his second year of music lessons as he strives to master the 5-string banjo. He will never be another Pete Seeger, but at least he can see some light at the end of his musical tunnel. As his instructor Eric Nagler once said, "You may never make it to Carnegie Hall, but as long as you enjoy what you are doing, that's what counts."

For exercise Clare attended classes in Nordic walking. He attends a monthly book club at BookLore and his purchase of books from that same store continues to help keep the store's owner Nancy Frater financially solvent.

AcKNoWLedgeMeNtS

I wish to thank Gloria Nye of Spiral Press for editing this masterpiece and pulling together its illustrations into publishable form, and Gus Dickson for photos of the author and helping with the cover design.   In this novel I have drawn on the lives of various folks that I've known over the years and I have included many of their insights into living a good life. It would be remiss of me not to acknowledge the influence of my parents who unknowingly provided me with the inspiration for some of the characters of this novel. Their philosophies greatly shaped my writing of this work.

Gloria Nye, my wife Dorothy and friends Len and Mary Johnson of Orillia read and provided welcome insights to the original unedited manuscript before I made major revisions based on their suggestions. I attended several workshops sponsored by the Town of Orangeville Public Library and presented by author Richard Scarsbrook. This also included an informative one-on-one session with Richard. I have incorporated suggestion made during those various happenings into this novel. Therefore I thank the Orangeville Library Board and Richard Scarsbrook for their interest in my writing.

QUotatioNS:

The quotations used in this novel have come from years of collecting ones which I have found particularly entertaining or enlightening. Some are from well-know sources and recognizable while others are more obscure and in some cases have been altered by someone from their original form. Due to the varied methods of transmission whether it be by word-of-mouth, collected on scraps of paper or from farm magazines, newspapers, out-of-print publications, or books of collections of quotations, I apologize for being unable to assign an originator for those that I've used (other than the hypothetical characters which appear in this novel). There are even a few of my originals but I've lost track of which ones are.

"Set yer sights on joinin' the author in his hunt to
bag a new Porcupine Junction tale
to mount on his trophy wall."